LATIN AMERICAN DICTIONARY SERIES
Edited by A. Curtis Wilgus

1. Moore, Richard E.   *Historical Dictionary of Guatemala.*   1967

2. Hedrick, Basil C. & Anne K.   *Historical Dictionary of Panama.*   1970

3. Rudolph, Donna Keyse & G. A.   *Historical Dictionary of Venezuela.*   1971

Historical Dictionary of Venezuela

by
Donna Keyse Rudolph
and G. A. Rudolph

Latin American Historical Dictionaries, No. 3

The Scarecrow Press, Inc.
Metuchen, N.J.   1971

Editor's Foreword

Venezuela has had an exciting history, and is the
homeland of many famous men, and some women, known
throughout the world. Its natural wealth has been the envy
of some of its continental neighbors, while its domestic and
foreign policies have often been criticized by governments with
less stability and more serious problems. Thus the prepara-
tion of an historical dictionary of this country has been a
real challenge; the question of what to omit and what to include is most perplexing, as the authors have discovered.
Fundamentally, their task has been to select topics on a
logical, comprehensive, and justifiable basis so that the result is a well-balanced dictionary instead of an encyclopedia.
Although perhaps not every compiler would have made the
same selections, the Rudolphs have been able to present a
useful guide which will be welcomed by those seeking brief
and concise knowledge about many aspects of Venezuelan
history. This information should be supplemented from a
variety of sources, some of which are listed in the bibli-
ography at the end of the volume.

Dr. and Mrs. Rudolph are a family team with individual and collective interests in Latin America extending
over a period of several years. Mrs. Rudolph has served
as librarian at Harvard University, Ohio University, and the
Universidad Nacional Mayor de San Marcos, Lima, Peru.
She has taught Spanish in the Department of Modern Languages
at Kansas State University and at present reviews books on
Latin American history for Choice.

Dr. Rudolph's interests have been somewhat more
varied. He too reviews books for Choice, but in the field
of philosophy. He has published articles in Spanish and
English on aesthetics and librarianship, and bibliographies
on cookery and Linneana. He has served as librarian at
Ohio University and at Kansas State University and was a
Fulbright consultant in librarianship at the Universidad
Nacional Mayor de San Marcos, Lima. He was a library
consultant also for the University of Kansas at the Universidad de Oriente, Cumaná, Venezuela. At present Dr.

Rudolph is Director of Libraries at the Virginia Polytechnic Institute and State University, Blackburg, Virginia.

A. Curtis Wilgus
Emeritus Director
School of Inter-American Studies
University of Florida

Introduction

Every effort has been made to include information concerning all of the important events and persons that relate to the history of Venezuela through 1969. It proved almost impossible to include only events, inasmuch as persons obviously are responsible for bringing events to pass. Perhaps, as a result, there is an emphasis on the names of people who helped create the history of Venezuela. Nevertheless, this book is not a biography of Venezuelan personages. It is an historical dictionary.

The entries are alphabetically arranged, with cross-references from the variants and from the acronymic initials of certain organizations and political parties. Under the entry "Presidents" there was an attempt to list therein all of the rulers of the country since the establishment of the Fourth Republic in 1831. All of the de facto rulers, during the periods when the presidents were out of the country or were fighting some rebel, could not be listed inasmuch as the list would have been too long and not within the scope of this volume.

Information concerning historical Venezuela can be located herein under either the name of the event or the name of the significant individual involved, or under both entries. Very few geographical entries have been included. It is believed that the reader will be able to locate any information that he desires concerning the history of Venezuela and that the information herein contained will solve his initial quest for such knowledge, allowing him to search, at a later time, for more complete information, should he so wish.

A.D.   see ACCION DEMOCRATICA

A.V.I.   see ASOCIACION VENEZOLANA INDEPENDIENTE

A.V.P.   see ASOCIACION VENEZOLANA DE PERIODISTAS

ABALOS, JUAN; or JOSE DE ABALOS; or JOSE DE AVALOS.
First Intendant, 1776-1783.   Intendancy was established
specifically to stimulate agriculture.   Indendant was
appointed by the King and was granted more power
than the governor.   Agriculture, trade, colonization,
and the administration of public income and military
budgets were all under the jurisdiction of the Intendant.   Abalos was a man of great energy and in-
tegrity.

ABREU, OVIDIO M.   General.   Head of the government of
the State of Zamora for 18 years, more or less con-
secutively.   He was a Liberal member of the Congress
of 1890.

ACADEMIA DE ARTES PLASTICAS.   In 1912, El Instituto de
Música y Declamación became two organizations: El
Conservatorio de Música y Declamación, and La
Academia de Artes Plásticas.   They were differenti-
ated, at least nominally, by the decree of 11 April
1913.   They were physically separated in 1936.

ACADEMIA DE CIENCIAS FISICAS Y NATURALES.   Founded
in Caracas in 1857, its president was Carlos Arvelo
and the vice-president was Antonio José Rodríguez.
The academy published Eco científico de Venezuela
which printed medical articles as well as articles
for the natural sciences.

ACADEMIA DE MATEMATICAS.   Founded by Juan Manuel
Cagigal, it was created by decree on 14 October
1830, but it was installed publicly on 4 November
1831.   Its directors were Juan Manuel Cagigal and

Rafael Acevedo. Guzmán Blanco joined it to the Universidad Central. Its last director was Juan José Aguerrevere. See also ACADEMIA MILITAR DE MATEMATICAS.

ACADEMIA DE MEDICINA. Founded by Luis Razetti in 1904 to replace El Colegio de Médicos which was inaugurated in 1902.

ACADEMIA MILITAR DE MATEMATICAS. Founded by decree on 14 October 1830. The installation was 4 November 1831 under the directorship of Juan Manuel Cagigal. By decree on 19 November 1872 Guzmán Blanco closed the institution and joined it to the Universidad Central. The last director was Juan José Aguerrevere. General Alcántara in 1877 reestablished the academy, but Guzmán Blanco in 1879 closed it again, passing it once more to the university.

ACADEMIA NACIONAL DE LA HISTORIA. Founded in 1888 by Rojas Paúl.

ACADEMIA VENEZOLANA DE LA LENGUA, CORRESPONDIENTE DE LA ESPAÑOLA. Founded by Guzmán Blanco in 1883. He was also the first director.

ACADEMICAS DE BELLAS ARTES. The Disputación Provincial de Caracas founded in December, 1849, La Academia de Bellas Artes. Antonio José Carranza was the first director. Guzmán Blanco by decree on 7 May 1870 created El Conservatorio de Bellas Artes. Felipe Larrazábal was named director. By the decree of 8 April 1877, El Instituto de Bellas Artes was created and Ramón de la Plaza named as director. Guzmán Blanco created by the decree of 4 August 1887, La Academia Nacional de Bellas Artes. Emilio J. Mauri was the director. In 1897 the academy was named by decree El Instituto de Bellas Artes. In 1904 it became Academia again and in 1905 Instituto. In 1912, El Instituto de Bellas Artes separated into La Academia de Artes Plásticas and El Conservatorio de Música y Declamación. The decree of 11 April 1913 differentiated the two areas, at least nominally. They were physically separated in 1936. After Mauri died in 1909, Antonio Herrera Tor was director until his death 26 June 1914.

ACCION DEMOCRATICA.   Original party was formed in 1931
in Barranquilla, Colombia, when exiles met to defeat
Gómez.   The 1931 leaders were Marxist and revolutionary.   There was a common cause during 1936-1937
with the Communist Party, but after 1937 the international communists withdrew and the Partido Democrático Nacional became a nationalist party.   The
leaders were Rómulo Betancourt, Gonzalo Barrios,
Raúl Leoni, and Luis Beltrán Prieto Figueroa.   The
party went underground during 1937-1941.   The name,
Acción Democrática, was legally recognized on 13
September 1941.   They supported Rómulo Gallegos for
the Presidency in 1941, but he was defeated when
Congress met in joint session.   Supported by junior
military officers as well as by students and reformers,
Betancourt took over the government in 1945 when
Medina was overthrown.   He and the Junta ruled by
decree for two years.   Universal suffrage for 18-year-
olds was granted in March, 1946.   Rómulo Gallegos
was elected President in December 1947 and took office on 14 February 1948, but the army overthrew
the government on 24 November 1948.   The main
interest of the party had been a democratic constitution which provided for the direct election of the
President for a limited period of time.   This constitution was adopted in 1947, but was revoked by the
military Junta in favor of the 1936 constitution.   The
party reorganized after Pérez Jiménez was overthrown,
and successfully maintained power.   Betancourt served
as President, 1959-1964.   The short-lived experiment
with U.R.D. in tri-party coalition ended in 1960 when
younger leaders split, forming Movimiento de Izquierda
Revolucionaria.   In 1961-1962 Acción Democrática also
split into A.D.-Vieja Guardia, led by the original
leaders, and into A.D.-Ars or A.D.-OP (Acción
Democrática en Oposición), led by Raúl Ramos
Jiménez.   Raúl Leoni was elected President in
December, 1963, serving 1964-1968.   There was an
attempted coalition with U.R.D. and F.N.D., but in
1966 F.N.D. dropped out.   In general Acción Democrática has been known for its economy of moderate
nationalism and for its state welfarism.   Its government has focussed attention on reforms in agriculture,
housing, education, and in passing laws concerning
civil standards and social security.   It opened immigration to European displaced persons.   In 1968 Luis
Beltrán Prieto Figueroa formed People's Electoral
Movement with Jesús Angel Paz Galarraga.

ACCION EN VENEZUELA. A private, nonprofit, urban
community-development organization.

ACCION VENEZOLANA INDEPENDIENTE see ASOCIACION
VENEZOLANA INDEPENDIENTE.

ACHAGUA INDIANS. They occupied the territory now com-
prising the states of Bolívar, Guárico, and Barinas.
These Indians had the vision of El Dorado: Manoa,
the hidden lake city with gold turrets, the domain of
King Paititi. Achagua villages resembled eastern
North American Indian villages. The Indians practiced infanticide, killing the first-born daughter.
Their weapon was the bow and arrow, the latter being tipped with curare. They worshipped various
gods, and revered lakes. They had no idols.

ACLAMACION. Name of the last term of Guzmán Blanco,
1886-1888. It was taken from El Libro de la Aclamación Nacional which begged him to stand for election again.

ACOSTA, CECILIO, 1819-1881. Poet, orator, essayist,
philosopher, legislator, he taught political economics.
He was an adversary of Guzmán Blanco. His
Reflections on History and Political Parties as well
as his studies on immigration are important.

ADMIRABLE CAMPAIGN. The name given to the campaign
fought by Bolívar's army in 1813 in freeing
Venezuela. His army consisted of Girardot as commander of the First Division, D'Elhuyar as his
second-in-command. Ribas commanded the rearguard.
Tejada was in command of the artillery. Urdaneta
was Bolívar's second-in-command. The main battles
of the campaign were Niquitao near Trujillo where
Ribas on July 2nd defeated Colonel José Martí; los
Horcones, near Barquisimeto, which Ribas fought on
July 22nd; and Bolívar's victory at Taguanes on
July 31st (between San Carlos and Valencia) where he
defeated Colonel Izquierdo.

ADRIANI, ALBERTO. Minister of Agriculture and later
Minister of the Treasury for López Contreras in 1936.

AGRARIAN REFORM. The Agrarian Reform Law was signed
by President Rómulo Gallegos on 18 October 1948. It

created the National Agrarian Institute which was supported by 3 per cent of the governmental budget. The major task of the Institute was to expropriate idle or unwisely used lands of over 300 hectares, to compensate, and to redistribute the property. The Agrarian Reform Law was enacted on 5 March 1960, recreating the National Agrarian Institute which then began breaking up large landed estates and redistributing the land to the property-less peasantry. Idle lands were taxed and the expropriation of large farms was sanctioned.

AGUILERA, JOSE ONOFRE. General. Secretary to Andueza Palacio in 1890. He was Deputy from Zamora in the Congress of 1890, although by 1891 he had still remained in Lara as an official of the government of Tesalio R. Fortoul.

AGUIRRE, LOPE DE. One of Pizarro's conquistadores who left Perú in 1560 bound for El Dorado. He arrived in 1561 at Margarita Island where his band plundered Asunción and stole gold and silver from the Real Hacienda. The band then sacked Borburata and marched to Valencia. His men deserted at Nueva Segovia (Barquisimeto). He stabbed his daughter in order to save her from rape and reprisals, and then he surrendered. He was shot and his dismembered body was fed to the dogs.

ALBERRO, FRANCISCO DE. Governor in 1679 who saw that Indian women were freed from labor, that the men only worked three days per week, and that a small wage was paid to the Indians. He also freed the Indians who had been brought forcibly from the llanos and made to perform slave labor.

ALFINGER, AMBROSIO; or AMBROSIO EHINGER. Coro's first German Governor under the Welsers. He sacked the area around Lake Maracaibo and the region west of it, leaving a trail of dead Indians, burned villages and ruined crops. In 1530 he sent 25 men back to Coro while he waited in eastern Colombia for them to return. Captain Iñigo de Vascuña and party, except Francisco Martín, were never heard of again. A year later Alfinger headed south. Near present-day Cucutá, Colombia, he was wounded by Indians and died. His men returned to Coro.

ALIANZA POPULAR INDEPENDIENTE.   Formed in 1966 from
a group which splintered from the F.N.D.

ALVARADO, LISANDRO, 1858-1929.   He revealed the social
content of mid-nineteenth century Federalist War
period in La Historia de la revolución.   He had talked
with veterans, had studied the battlefields, and had
collected anecdotes in order to supplement the information that he had obtained from books, periodicals, and
letters.   He also wrote extensively on local ethnography
and folklore.   He fought alongside Joaquín Crespo in
1890.

ALVARADO, DR. VICTOR.   Deputy from Carabobo in the
Congress of 1890.   He was born in Guanare and
studied law in Mérida.   Guzmán proposed a ministry
to him, but he refused.   He was named as Deputy to
the Congress, but did not attend.   He was reputed to
have one of the best libraries in Venezuela.

AMERICAN CONFEDERATION OF VENEZUELA.   The name
of the First Republic.   It comprised the united provinces of Caracas, Cumaná, Barinas, Margarita,
Barcelona, Mérida, and Trujillo.   Valencia became
the federal capital in October, 1811.   There was a
new constitution and a provisional government, the
latter being elected in March, 1812.   The political
situation became complicated until the point was
reached where the Executive could only govern
dictatorially.   The federal nature of the constitution
contributed to the lack of cohesion of the government.
The causes for the government's defeat were lack of
military training and lack of enthusiasm by the people.

AMPUES, JUAN DE; or JUAN DE AMPIES.   In 1527 he land-
ed on Paraguaná Peninsula with 60 men and on 27
July 1527 laid out the city to be called Santa Ana de
Coro.   It was the first European settlement in western
Venezuela, and was intended to serve as a check
point for the control of the Indian slave trade.   In 1528
Charles V replaced him.

ANDRADE, IGNACIO.   General.   He was President for 18
months, February 1898-22 October 1899, after the
death of Crespo.   During his administration there was
continual revolution.   General Ramón Guerra defeated
and imprisoned Hernández.   Then Guerra revolted.

Cipriano Castro and Juan Vicente Gómez fought against
Andrade. After the battle of Tocuyito, Andrade began
to lose supporters. Cipriano Castro entered Caracas
on 22 October 1899.

ANDRESOTE. Zambo (Indian and Negro half-breed) who led
revolt against Compañía Guipuzcoana in 1730-1733.
He was a smuggler who eventually had a small army
of escaped slaves. In 1731 he was outlawed for being
a rebel, armed brigand, murderer, traitor, and smuggler. He defeated the government forces in July,
1732, but was himself defeated in January, 1733. He
then sought refuge in Curaçao.

ANDUEZA PALACIO, RAIMUNDO. He was President, 1890-
1892. He was born 6 February 1843 in Guanare,
Zamora. He was Deputy to the legislative assembly
of Portugueza. In 1866 he was Edecán, then the private secretary of the President of the Republic. In
1868 he was secretary of the municipal government of
Caracas. He was with General Pedro Manuel Rojas,
the military chief of the East, as subsecretary, at the
conferences of La Miel. Before 1878 he had been a
member of the legislature for four years, twice being
President of the Cámara de Diputados. In 1878 he
was Foreign Minister and became candidate for President. He had been Minister of the Interior, Foreign
Minister, and Chancellor of the Exchequer, and had
more than once been a member of the Federal Council. He was an editor along with Dr. Laureano Villanueva, of El Pabellón de abril and El Demócrata, during the administration of General Alcántara. He
wanted to reform the constitution to allow a longer
presidential term and wanted direct elections by the
people. Rojas Paúl was expelled by him in 1891.
The June, 1892 revolution caused him to resign, leaving the country in a state of war and in economic cri-
sis.

ANGOSTURA. Colonial city on the Orinoco in the present
State of Bolívar. It was notable in revolutionary history as the place where patriot forces first gained
control of the lower Orinoco region and, later, as the
seat of the congress that devised under Bolívar the
Angostura Constitution of 1819. After independence,
the city was renamed Ciudad Bolívar.

ANGOSTURA, CONGRESS OF. On 15 February 1819 delegates met at Angostura, confirming Bolívar as the
commander in chief of the patriot army and as President of the Republic of Venezuela. Zea was confirmed as Vice-President, Palacio Fajardo was confirmed as Secretary of State and Treasury, Briceño
Méndez was confirmed as Secretary of War and Navy,
and Diego Bautista Urbaneja was confirmed as Secretary of the Interior and Justice. The constitution was
adopted 15 August 1819. In September Arismendi replaced Zea as Vice-President. On 16 December the
Congress created Gran Colombia and Bolívar was
chosen as President. The political foundation of the
Third Republic was thus laid. Bolívar's address was
his second serious political announcement. He spoke
for a hereditary senate, elected by the congress,
which would be composed of first generation liberators
or of men who were especially trained. He opposed
federalism and called for laws guaranteeing civil lib-
erties and endorsing military actions to free the
slaves. The new government was composed of Cundinamarca (Colombia), Quito (Ecuador), and Caracas
(Venezuela). The Congress was dissolved on 15 January 1820.

ANTHEM. Gloria al Bravo Pueblo is the national anthem.
It was adopted by the decree of Antonio Guzmán
Blanco in 1881. The lyrics were written by Vicente
Salías and the music by Juan Landaeta, both impris-
oned and then shot in 1814 during the war for inde-
pendence.

ANTOÑANZAS, EUSEBIO. Royalist commander during the
Wars of Independence. On 20 May 1812 he captured
Calabozo, releasing José Tomás Boves who then joined
the Royalist forces.

ANZOATEGUI, JOSE ANTONIO, 1789-1819. After being freed
from captivity in May, 1813, he fought in army of
Campos Elias in August. He fought at the first battle of
La Puerta and then at Mosquiteros in 1813. He went
with Bolívar to Nueva Granada, then to Haiti. In 1818
as chief of the guard of honor of the supreme chief,
he took part in the battle of Calabozo, of El Sombrero,
and in the third La Puerta. He became a general of
brigade in 1818. In the campaign of 1819 he became
chief of the Army of the East. He fought along with

Bolívar in Nueva Granada in 1819, dying there on 15 November 1819.

ARANDA, FRANCISCO, 1798-1873. After Carabobo he was secretary to Vice President Soublette. In 1828 he attended the convention at Ocaña, as Deputy from Venezuela. In 1829 he was elected Deputy from Caracas to the Admirable Congress in Bogotá which was held in 1830. He was a member of the Congress of 1834. In 1841 he was the Chancellor of the Exchequer and Minister of Foreign Relations, posts which he also held in 1843. He was a member of the Congresses of 1847, 1848, and 1851. In 1851 he became Secretary of State with the portfolios of Interior and Justice. In 1855 he was Secretary of the Interior and Justice; then Ambassador to Washington. In 1856 he was Secretary of Interior and Justice. In 1859 he was Secretary of the Interior.

ARANGUREN, ANTONIO. In 1874 Guzmán Blanco under the pretext that enemies at Curaçao were smuggling arms to Venezuela, closed the ports of Maracaibo and La Vela de Coro. Then he awarded the navigation monopoly to Francisco Fossi and Antonio Aranguren who were both his partners.

ARANGUREN, PEDRO. In the War of Federation he was so bad-tempered as a government commander that his own soldiers shot him without trial.

ARAUJO, JUAN BAUTISTA. General and conservative caudillo of Los Andes for many years. He was a member of the red division of the anti-Liberal army in the War of the Federation, but had a falling out with Guzmán in 1887. He was a Senator to the Congress from Los Andes in 1890.

ARAURE, WARS OF. Great victory in the War for Independence. On 5 December 1813 Bolívar led 2,500 soldiers against 5,000 Royalists, composed of troops of Governor Cevallos from Coro and of an army of the llaneros. The victory gave Bolívar a two-month respite, attempting to save the Second Republic.

ARCAYA, PEDRO MANUEL, 1874- . Gómez's ambassador to the United States who wrote Venezuela y su actual régimen, defending Gómez. He was president of the

Coro Municipal Council (1896-1904), supreme court judge (1909-1913), national Attorney General (1913-1914), Minister of the Interior (1914-1917, 1924-1927), Senator (1918-1922) and an ambassador (1922-1924, 1930-1936).

ARCHBISHOPRIC OF VENEZUELA. Seat was in Caracas. The diocese is limited on the north from the Unare River to the jurisdiction of Coro; on the east by the province of Cumaná; on the south by the Orinoco; and to the west by the bishopric of Mérida. It became an archbishopric in 1803. The first bishop of Venezuela was Rodrigo de Bastidas at the See of Coro in 1531. In 1638 the See was transferred to Caracas. Margarita, Trinidad, Cumaná, and Guayana became at that time dependent upon the See of Puerto Rico while Los Andes belonged to the Archdiocese of Bogotá. In 1777 Mérida became bishopric under jurisdiction of Bogotá. In 1790 Guayana became diocese under archdiocese of Santo Domingo. In 1796 the island of Santo Domingo became French property so Caracas was made archbishopric in 1803 with bishops of Guayana and Mérida under its authority.

AREVALO CEDEÑO, EMILIO. General who raided Venezuela seven times during regime of Gómez. In 1914 he was in Guárico; in 1918 in the Arauco region; and in 1921 in the Amazonas Territory. His last attempt was an invasion from Colombia. In the Amazonas, he captured the headquarters of Funes, a murderer, whom he tried and shot. His unsuccessful march into Apure State ended with Arévalo's retreat into Colombia.

ARISMENDI, JUAN BAUTISTA, 1775-1841. General in Chief. He was governor of Margarita in 1814 when it was the last piece of patriot territory. In 1816 the island was still partly under his command. In November, 1816 he invited the patriots to take refuge on the island. At the beginning of 1817 he left for the mainland when he took part in the 1817 Guayana campaign. He became Vice-President in September, 1819, replacing Zea. He returned to Margarita in 1821. He became commander of the armies of the Department of Orinoco in 1824. In 1829 he went to Caracas as chief of the High Police.

ARISTEGUIETA, JESUS MARIA. General and Senator for

Los Andes in the Congress of 1890. He was Liberal
Minister of Public Works during War of Federation.

ARMED FORCES FOR NATIONAL LIBERATION see FUERZAS
ARMADAS DE LIBERACION NACIONAL

ARRAIZ, ANTONIO, 1903- . In Puros hombres, 1938, he
explored the repressive atmosphere and the rural pov-
erty of the Gómez period. As a poet, his "Aspero, "
1924, used free verse and the lyric grandeur that is
reminiscent of Whitman. He was a political opponent
of Gómez, and the founder and editor of the Caracas
daily, El Nacional. His "Unfinished Symphony" is
often considered among the country's best poems.

ARRIETA, DR. DIOGENES A. Deputy for Los Andes in the
Congress of 1890. He was originally a Colombian
newspaperman who was known for his biographies of
political personages of Venezuela. He supported
Rojas Paúl for president.

ARTEAGA, CAPITAN MARTIN DE. He came with Abrosio
de Alfinger to Venezuela in 1528. He went with
Federmann toward Barquisimeto in 1530 from Coro.
He also went on the great expedition of Espira. In
1540 he went with Felipe de Hutten in search of El
Dorado. He lived in Coro 1570-1580.

ARVELO, DR. CARLOS. He was an unsuccessful candidate
for president against Alcántara. He was a senator
for Lara in the Congress of 1890 and a Liberal medical doctor who lived in Santo Domingo once where he
had been associated with President Lilís in the construction of a public market.

ARVELO, DR. FERNANDO. As a Senator for Bermúdez in
the Congress of 1890, he was a member of the Liberal Party. He was Minister of Interior in the time of
Falcón, when he ignored the individual guarantees of
the Constitution of 1864.

ARVELO, RAFAEL, 1814-1878. First satirical poet who
entered politics supporting Guzmán and later Monagas.
He was a Deputy to Congress, a governor of a province, Minister of State, and a provisional President
of the Republic in 1867.

ASOCIACION DE EMPLEADOS PUBLICOS. As a white-collar government workers group not entitled to union status by law, it still lobbies for employee benefits.

ASOCIACION PRO-VENEZUELA. Formed in 1958 to represent primarily the interest of the middle-level industries and businessmen.

ASOCIACION VENEZOLANA DE PERIODISTAS. White-collar journalist union.

ASOCIACION VENEZOLANA INDEPENDIENTE. Formed in 1962 to provide financial support for campaigns of various political parties in exchange for influence over the selection of candidates as an assurance that the business community's interest will be taken into account in the government. It is unregistered as a party, but it is capable of strong pressure group action. It is also known as Acción Venezolana Independiente.

AUDIENCIA OF CARACAS. Installed 19 July 1787 as the supreme judicial court, also advising the Captain-General on administrative matters. It was established in Caracas in 1786 by Charles III.

AUDIENCIA OF SANTA FE (DE BOGOTA). In 1550 it was given jurisdiction over Nueva Granada. It became a Viceroyalty in 1718. Venezuela was under the Audiencia in 1717-1723 and in 1739-1742.

AUDIENCIA OF SANTO DOMINGO. Venezuela was under authority until 1717. When Viceroyalty of Bogotá was suppressed in 1723, Venezuela returned to this jurisdiction, remaining until 1739 when it was returned to the authority of Bogotá. It was returned again during 1742-1786. In 1777 Charles III decreed the unification of the political, economic and military affairs in all the provinces of Venezuela and placed them under the Audiencia of Santo Domingo for judicial matters.

AUSTRIA, JOSE, 1791-1863. Writer and military officer. He served under Miranda, Urdaneta, Campos Elías, Bolívar, Bermúdez, Justo Briceño, and Páez; he also served in the federal wars. In 1846 he was chief official of the Ministry of War. In 1857 he was a member of the Council of Government of the Republic. In 1858 he was Minister of War and became a General of Division.

-B-

B. A. N. see BLOQUE DE ACCION NACIONAL

B. A. P. see BANCO AGRICOLA Y PECUARIO

BANCO AGRICOLA Y PECUARIO. Government banking entity with wide powers in the field of agricultural reform, development, credits and imports.

BAPTISTA, DR. EUSEBIO. In 1892 his nomination as Senator was the act around which the revolt occurred.
He was opposed by President Andueza Palacio.

BAPTISTA, DR. LEOPOLDO. Son of the President of Los
Andes and a Deputy for Los Andes in the Congress
of 1890. He had helped Gómez depose Castro. He
was once secretary to Juan Vicente Gómez.

BARALT, RAFAEL MARIA, 1810-1860. Classical historian
of the independence period who was famous for his
Resumen de la historia antigua y moderna de Venezuela. In spite of an anti-Spanish attitude, he spent
the latter part of his life in Spain and received membership into the Royal Academy of History. His work
is regarded in Venezuela as the principal authority of
the period.

BARBULA, BATTLE OF. 30 September 1813 Republican
victory which was one of Monteverde's last battles.
He had marched from Puerto Cabello with reinforcements of 1, 200 men towards Caracas when he was
confronted by patriots.

BARQUISIMETO see NUEVA SEGOVIA

BARRIOS, GONZALO. Member of the Junta Revolucionaria
in 1945. The Junta had promised universal suffrage,
direct election of the President, and a new constitution. He was also secretary to the Presidency of
Venezuela, 1948. He was Minister of Interior Relations in 1964 and A. D. candidate for President in
1968.

BASTIDAS, RODRIGO DE. In 1500 he set out on a long voyage, anchoring at many points along the Venezuelan coast in order to load brazilwood, to trade for gold and pearls, and to study the land. He was accompanied by Juan de la Cosa. He reached as far west as Santa Marta and Cartagena.

BASTIDAS, RODRIGO DE. First bishop of Coro, who arrived in 1536 although he was given the See in 1531. In 1540 the Audiencia of Hispaniola found him the logical choice for the interim governorship. He had a strong influence in the colony and had supported the Welser administration. His lieutenant was Philip von Hutten.

BATALLA, FRANCISCO. General. Rich, but honorable official who was noted for his brilliant attire when he was President of the State of Zamora. He was Deputy for Zamora in the Congress of 1890.

BELLO, DIONISIA. Wife of an Italian merchant, she was carried off to "La Mulera" by Gómez when he was 28 years old. She mothered 7 of his 14 recognized illegitimate children.

BELLO LOPEZ, ANDRES, 1781-1865. Poet, lawyer, educator, grammarian, publicist, journalist, and statesman. As a student he was influenced by von Humboldt. As editor in 1808 of the Gaceta de Caracas, he used its press to print the first book in Venezuela, Calendario manual y guía universal de forasteros en Caracas para 1810. He accompanied Bolívar to Great Britain in 1810 and remained there until 1829 as the Venezuelan representative in London. During this period he wrote "Alocución a la poesía" and "A la agricultura de la Zona Tórrida" which is considered the first expression of national literature and the nationalist theme. He later went to Chile, working for the Chilean government, and became Rector of the Universidad de Chile in 1843. In 1843 he wrote Teoría del entendimiento; filosofía del entendimiento which appeared posthumously.

BERMUDEZ. State named by Guzmán who was flattering Pedro Vallenilla in so doing.

BERMUDEZ, BERNARDO. Along with Mariño and Piar he
refused to recognize the command of Bolívar in 1816.
At the beginning of 1817 he was reconciled with Bolívar and fought near Cumaná in the east. He became
governor for Cumaná in 1818.

BERMUDEZ, JOSE FRANCISCO, 1782-1831. Patriot dating
from 1810 and ally of Mariño in the war of the Second Republic. In 1814 he fought at Bocachica, Areo,
the first battle of Carabobo, and the second battle of
La Puerta. There was a rivalry with Bolívar, but it
was reconciled in 1817. He fought in the east 1817-
1818 and was named General-in-Chief of the Army of
the East. In 1823 he fought against Morales, and
supported the constitution in 1826. He opposed the
separatist movement in 1830 and was assassinated on
15 December 1831.

BERMUDEZ, MANUEL MARIA. General; poet; gourmet;
generous, wordy, and occasional secretary to Guzmán
Blanco; Supreme Court Justice; and poor conspirator;
he was Deputy for Miranda in the Congress of 1890.

BETANCOURT, ROMULO, 1908- . Generation of 1928. He
opposed Juan Vicente Gómez and was exiled in 1928.
A member of the Communist Party in Costa Rica in
1930, he later quit the party. He founded the newspaper Orve in 1936 in Venezuela. While underground
1936-1939 he organized El Partido Democrático Venezolano. He was exiled in 1940. In 1941 he was
founder and secretary general of Acción Democrática.
He was co-founder of the newspaper El País in 1943.
When U.P.M. and A.D. helped overthrow Medina
Angarita, he became President of the seven-man Junta,
1945-1947. He headed the delegation to the Conference
of Bogotá, the Ninth Pan American Conference, in
1948 and was exiled when the army overthrew the
government that same year. He returned in 1958 for
the elections and became President, as nominee of
Acción Democrática, on 13 February 1959, serving
until 1964.

BIAGGINI, ANGEL. When Medina Angarita in 1945 proposed
the candidacy of Angel Biaggini, one of his more col-
orless ministers, it appeared that Medina Angarita
wished to rule five more years with Biaggini as his
front. Acción Democrática formed an alliance then
with the military and overthrew the government. He

was secretary to the President of Venezuela in 1943 and Minister of Agriculture in 1945.

BLANCO, ANDRES ELOY, 1898-1955. Poet who brought back folk couplets and the romance of the Spanish tradition. He lacked ability for conceit and abstractions, but was rich in popular proverbs and myths which were presented in troubador style. He was president of the Constituent Assembly in 1947 and Minister of Foreign Relations in 1948.

BLANCO, CARLOTA. Antonio Leocadio Guzmán contrived to woo Carlota Blanco who was related on both sides to the Bolívars, María Antonia Bolívar, sister of Simón, being her godmother. She married Guzmán on 30 September 1828. Antonio Guzmán Blanco was born five months later.

BLANCO, EDUARDO, 1839-1912. As one of the most brilliant figures in Venezuelan letters, he is most famous for Venezuela heróica, the epic portrayal of glory of Bolívar and the War of Independence. At one time he was secretary to Páez. He was also Minister of Public Instruction and a charter member of the Academia Nacional de la Historia in 1889.

BLANCO, JERONIMO E., 1823-1865. Minor humanist writer.

BLANCO, JOSE FELIX, 1782-1872. It was he who made possible the presence of Madariaga on 19 April 1810. Serving with the various armies of the Marquis de Toro, Urdaneta, Mariño, and Bolívar, he fought in the Wars of Independence. He occupied various government positions, including a portfolio in the government of José Tadeo Monagas. In 1863 he was rehabilitated by Pope Gregorio XVI and made the Archbishop of Caracas.

BLANCO FOMBONA, RUFINO, 1874-1944. Member of the Generation of '95, he is one of the more important Venezuelan literary persons of the 19th and 20th centuries. Beginning with the modernist movement of El Cojo Ilustrado and the Cosmópolis groups, he turned to blunt prose for the portrayals of contemporary life. His dynamic, almost journalistic style, best in short stories, recreated familiar persons and places. He used satire and caricature in waging per-

sonal war against Juan Vicente Gómez.   His works
include: Cuentos de poeta (1900), El Hombre de
hierro (1907), Cantos de la prisión y del destierro
(1911), El Hombre de oro (1932), and El Secreto de
la felicidad (1932).   He was a strong opponent of Yan-
kee imperialism.

BLOQUE DE ABRIL.   Party in opposition to the government
during time following the death of Gómez.   It declared
a general strike after the massacre in Plaza Bolívar
on 14 February 1936.

BLOQUE DE ACCION NACIONAL.   Storm troopers of the
conservative forces in 1936, it was forced underground.   The original name was Acción Nacional.

BLUE REVOLUTION OF 1868-1869.   Mounted under the leadership of José Tadeo Monagas and Páez, it was re-
portedly the work of the propertied element who pos-
sessed 85% of the wealth.   The name of the revolution
comes from the color of the flag which was carried.
The overthrow of the Federalist government of General
Juan Falcón was followed by the election in 1868 of
José Tadeo Monagas as President for the third time.
The coalition of Liberals and Conservatives now supported Monagas, although ten years previously they
had ousted him.   Monagas died in November, 1868 and
Ruperto Monagas was chosen to succeed his father.
The Liberals broke with the Conservatives and rallied
around Guzmán Blanco; Generals Pulido, Crespo,
Salazar, and Colina asking him to lead them.   The
forces of Regeneration, as they called themselves,
took Caracas on 27 April 1870, unseating the Blues.

BOLET PERAZA, NICANOR, 1838-1906.   The best of the
Venezuelan costumbrismo, he was poet, writer, publisher, dramatist, as well as a politician.   In the
wars of 1858, he was a Federalist.

BOLIVAR, JUAN VICENTE,   -1786.   Father of Simón Bolívar and three other children.   His wife was Doña
María de la Concepción de Palacios y Blanco.   He left
258,000 pesos, two cacao plantations, thirteen houses
in Caracas and la Guaira, two country estates, a
plantation at San Mateo, one indigo ranch, three cattle ranches, a copper mine, and thousands of slaves.

BOLIVAR, SIMON, 1783-1830.   Born in Caracas on 24 July
1783, he was the youngest of four children.   He was
first tutored by Miguel José Sanz, and then by Carlos
Palacios.   Although Andrés Bello was his teacher, he
was most influenced by Simón Carreño (alias Rodríguez, alias Robinson).   Rodríguez fled Venezuela in
1797 after the abortive España revolt.   Bolívar went
to Europe in 1799.   He married María Teresa de
Toro y Alaysa and sailed for Venezuela in June, 1802.
Six months later she died of yellow fever.   Bolívar
sailed again for Europe and was reunited with Rodríguez.   He returned to Venezuela in 1807.   During the
First Republic he was sent as emissary to Great Britain in 1810.   At the fall of the First Republic he fled
from Venezuela in August, 1812.   He fought his way
back into western Venezuela from Colombia in 1813,
reaching Caracas on 7 August 1813.   He was given
the title El Libertador and proclaimed the Second Republic.   Forced into exile after the Second Republic
fell in 1814, his attempted landing on the coast in
1815 was defeated.   In 1817 an invasion was launched
from Haiti and Angostura on the Orinoco was seized.
The Congress of Angostura in 1819 adopted the new
constitution and elected Bolívar President of the Third
Republic.   After the defeat of the Spanish army at
Boyacá, a truce was signed in 1820.   In June, 1821
he won a decisive battle at Carabobo.   The Congress
of Cúcuta was called in 1821.   The Republic of Gran
Colombia was announced, Bolívar being President and
Santander, Vice-President.   Afterwards Bolívar travelled south to free Ecuador, Perú, and Bolivia.   Venezuela broke from Gran Colombia in 1829.   Bolívar
died at Santa Marta, Colombia on 17 December 1830,
penniless and almost alone.

BOLIVARIANS.   The name of a group of quasi-professional
and profession-oriented officers whose expressed union
was based on a common staff training and experience
in warfare and administration outside of Venezuela.
While Bolívar lived, he was the focus of their activities.   After his death, the officers continued as a
loosely-knit team without a dominant figure.

BONTEMPS, JEAN DE.   French freebooter who arrived on
the Venezuelan coast in 1566, returning annually.   In
1570 he burned Borburata which act caused the citizens of Borburata to move away.

BORBURATA.   Town on the Caribbean, founded in 1548.   It
was sacked by Aguirre about 1561.   Hawkins sailed
into the Borburata harbor in 1565 and traded there.
In 1567 Captain Jacques Sorel threatened to burn the
city.   In the same year Nicholas Valliers did burn
the city.   It was burned again in 1570 by Jean de
Bontemps.   The citizens then packed up and moved
away.

BOUNDARY PROBLEMS WITH BRAZIL.   After several years
of negotiations a treaty was signed in May, 1859 providing a boundary that was satisfactory to both powers.
In the unexplored southwestern extremity of Venezuela
the last questions concerning the boundary between
Brazil and Venezuela were reached under the protocol
of 9 December 1905.

BOUNDARY PROBLEMS WITH BRITISH GUIANA.   Venezuela
claimed in 1830 that the eastern boundary was the
Essequibo River, but the Schomburgk Line of 1841 assigned the boundary as the mouth of the Orinoco.   In
1877 gold was discovered in the disputed area.   Since
Great Britain refused to have the dispute arbitrated,
Venezuela suspended diplomatic relations with Great
Britain in 1887.   In 1895 the United States declared
that Great Britain violated the Monroe Doctrine and
demanded that the dispute be arbitrated.   In 1899 the
arbitration tribunal decided upon a line which was
roughly that of the old Schomburgk Line except that
Venezuela obtained control of the mouth of the Orinoco
River.   Diplomatic relations were then renewed between Great Britain and Venezuela.

BOUNDARY PROBLEMS WITH COLOMBIA.   Under the 1842
treaty, Venezuela and Colombia had agreed to arbi-
trate the border claims.   In 1881 it was finally agreed
that the King of Spain should act as arbitrator.   Venezuela was claiming the territory of the Captaincy-
General of Caracas of 1810 and Colombia was claiming all of the old Vice-Royalty of Santa Fé de Bogotá.
The Spanish monarch in 1891 decided that the boundary
line would be drawn at the source of the Río de Oro.
In 1901 a committee completed its work on detailing
the boundary, but Venezuela rejected the findings.
For years the dispute continued while Swiss experts
attempted to find a satisfactory solution.   In 1941 mutual concessions were reached so that a boundary line

could be drawn. In November, 1952 Colombia also
recognized Venezuela's claim to sovereignty over the
Los Monjes Archipelago, just off the Goajira Peninsula.

BOVES, JOSE TOMAS, ca. 1770-1814. (Real surname
RODRIGUES). Spanish soldier who adopted the name
of Boves in honor of his benefactor who had him released in 1812 from a sentence of long imprisonment
at Puerto Cabello. During the War of Independence,
Boves recruited llaneros to fight for Spain. He was
known for his brutality towards the patriots. His
success was consequent upon the establishment of social democracy in his forces. He freed slaves and
promoted mixed breeds and mulattoes. He was defeated by Campos Elías at Mosquiteros on 14 October
1813, but he defeated Campos Elías at La Puerta on 3
February 1814. Although he could not dislodge Bolívar at the battle of San Mateo on 25 March 1814 and
although he lost to Mariño at Bocachica on 31 March
1814, Boves entered Valencia on 10 July 1814 and
Caracas on 16 July 1814. He afterwards set up a
dictatorship, ignoring the Spanish orders for Cajigal
to become Captain-General. In the guerrilla warfare
that followed the departure of Bolívar and Mariño,
Boves was wounded in the Cumaná region and died 5
December 1814.

BRICEÑO, ANTONIO NICOLAS, 1782-1813. One of the two
secretaries of the Congress of 1811 and one of the
three Substitutes of the provisional government of
March, 1812. He accompanied Bolívar to Nueva Granada in 1812. He signed the death agreement of 16
January 1813 in Cartagena. Captured in 1813, he was
executed with seven other patriots.

BRICEÑO, DR. SANTIAGO. With General Rosendo Medina
he organized a local revolution in 1878.

BRICEÑO AYESTARIAN, SANTIAGO. Teacher, surveyor,
merchant, publisher, and commodity dealer. In 1897
he left his militia unit and went into politics because
of the oppression he saw. He joined the Cipriano
Castro movement in 1898. He was named Jefe de
Alzamiento in his home district of Táchira. In 1899
he was promoted to general and became Supreme
Court Justice in 1900. He was President of the State

of Táchira in 1902.

BRICEÑO MENDEZ, PEDRO,   -1835.   Took part in the
    campaigns of 1813-1815.   He was secretary to Piar
    in 1817 and Secretary of War and Navy in 1819.   He
    accompanied Bolívar to Nueva Granada.   He fought at
    Carabobo in 1821.   During the early years of Gran
    Colombia he was an official.   He was secretary to
    Páez in 1828 and attended the Congress of Bogotá in
    1830.   He was a Senator in the Venezuelan Congress
    of 1835.

BRION, LUIS, 1782-1821.   Bankrupted Curaçao merchant who
    aided patriots in 1815 and 1816.   In 1817 he was the
    admiral who commanded the Haitian-supplied fleet
    which cleared the Orinoco of Spaniards.   In 1818 he
    was one of Bolívar's Council of Government and went
    to Nueva Granada with Bolívar.

BRITISH LEGION.   After the Napoleonic Wars ex-soldiers
    went to Venezuela in 1818-1819.   Although Venezuela
    was not what they had anticipated, these British sol-
    diers performed well in the Wars of Independence.
    They participated importantly in the second battle of
    Carabobo in 1821.

-C-

C.O.P.E.I.   see   COMITE POR ORGANIZACION POLITICA
    Y ELECTORAL INDEPENDIENTE

C.T.A.L.   see   CONFEDERACION DE TRABAJADORES DE
    AMERICA LATINA

C.T.V.   see   CONFEDERACION DE TRABAJADORES DE
    VENEZUELA

C.V.F.   see   CORPORACION VENEZOLANA DE FOMENTO

C.V.G.   see   CORPORACION VENEZOLANA DE GUAYANA

CABERRE INDIANS.   In pre-Columbian times, the area's
    principal manufacturers of curare which they made
    from swamp root.

CAGIGAL, JUAN MANUEL; or JUAN MANUEL DE CAJIGAL,

1803-1856.   General Páez by the decree of 26 October
1831 established La Academia de Matemáticas, the
first official institution to be devoted to such studies.
Cagígal was the first director.   The present observa-
tory is named for him.

CAJIGAL, JUAN MANUEL DE.   Governor of Cumaná in 1808.
In 1814 he was the choice of the Spanish authorities
to be Captain-General, but Boves ignored the orders.
He fought Bolívar at the first battle of Carabobo.   He
became Captain-General in April, 1815, but was soon
replaced by Morillo.

CALCAÑO, EDUARDO, 1831-1904.   During the regimes of
Guzmán Blanco, he was many times Minister of Foreign Affairs and also Ambassador to Spain.

CALCAÑO, JULIO, 1840-1918.   General.   Founder of La
Academia Venezolana de la Lengua, and the perpetual
secretary of that organization for a long period.

CALDERA RODRIGUEZ, RAFAEL, 1916- .   In 1936 he
organized Unión Nacional de Estudiantes which split
off from the F. E. V.   As head of COPEI, he sympa-
thized with the 1945 revolution, but he opposed the
new government's socialist policies.   The origins of
COPEI occurred when Caldera Rodríguez led a small
conservative schismatic group, associated with Andean
landholders and the Spanish Falange, in opposition to
López Contreras.   After October, 1945, he served as
Attorney-General for the Junta.   He formally founded
COPEI in 1946, attempting to broaden its base by
combining a religious appeal with moderate social-
welfare programs for the lower and middle income
groups.   In 1946 he resigned his cabinet post in order
to protest the violence that was done to his party.
Nominated by COPEI and the Democratic Republican
Union as their presidential candidate in 1947, he was
defeated by Gallegos.   He was candidate for president
in 1958, and in 1963.   He was elected President in
December, 1968 and was installed as the 43rd President on 11 March 1969.

CALZADA, SEBASTIAN DE LA.   Lieutenant to Morillo in
1818.

CAMEJO, PEDRO,   -1821.   As a llanero, he fought with

Páez until Carabobo where he was killed.   He was
called "Negro Primero."

CAMPO Y ESPINOZA, ALONSO DEL.   In 1669 he commanded the force that unsuccessfully attempted to
block Henry Morgan's exit from Lake Maracaibo after
Morgan had plundered Maracaibo and Gibraltar.

CAMPOS ELIAS, VICENTE, 1759-1814.   He came to Venezuela in 1792.   He fought and defeated Boves at
Mosquiteros on 14 October 1813.   A Spaniard by
birth, he had sworn to kill every Spaniard in Venezuela.   He was defeated by Boves at La Puerta on 3
February 1814.   He died of battle wounds on 16 March
1814.

CANNIBALISM.   The Spanish treated the Quiriquire as cannibals and burned a "C" in their flesh before selling
them as slaves, although there was no record of the
Quiriquire practicing cannibalism.   The Caquetío
tribe in the same area used to grind up the bones of
the dead and would consume the dust in drink.   The
Caribs did like roasted Arawak and were responsible
for the name "cannibal."   The Maracapana ate the
intestines of a captured chieftain.

CAPTAIN-GENERALCY.   Venezuela had first been established
as a separate Captain-Generalcy in 1731.   In the period 1740-1777 she was part of the Vice-Royalty of
New Granada.   The Captain-Generalcy of Caracas was
established on 8 September 1777.   It included most
of what is present day Venezuela.   The Captain-General was the chief authority and supreme military
commander.   The Intendant was the controller of economic and financial matters.   The Audiencia was the
supreme judicial court and was advisor to the Captain-General on administrative matters.   There were
seven Captains-General in Venezuela until the time
of Independence.

CAPUCHINS.   Along with the Franciscans the Capuchins established themselves in Cumaná in 1650.   In 1693
they were ordered to establish a mission in the Maracaibo district.   Two friars accomplished this in
1694.   Today the Capuchins have the Apostolic Vicariate of Machiques, working the Venezuelan section
of Guajira and also working Sierra de Perijá.   Since

1922 they have managed the Apostolic Vicariate of Caroní in the State of Bolívar and the vicariate in the Delta Amacuro Federal Territory until 1954.

CARABALLEDA, NUESTRA SEÑORA DE.   Francisco Fajardo founded a settlement called El Collado near the present-day La Guaira in 1562.   Guaicaipuro and the Teques Indians forced the Spanish to abandon El Collado.   In 1580 a Portuguese ship arrived at the port of Caraballeda carrying smallpox causing an epidemic among the Indians.   In 1586 the citizens of Caraballeda abandoned the settlement rather than permit the Governor to usurp the right to elect two members of their cabildo.

CARABOBO, FIRST BATTLE OF.   On 28 May 1814 Bolívar defeated Ceballos and Cajigal at Carabobo.   Afterwards Cajigal fled towards the Apure and Ceballos went west.

CARABOBO, SECOND BATTLE OF.   The battle on 24 June 1821 assured the independence of Venezuela.   Bolívar, Páez, Cedeño, Mariño, and Ambrosio Plaza with approximately 6,500 men attacked La Torre and 5,000 men on the plains of Carabobo.   Approximately 3,500 Spanish troops were killed or taken prisoner, the rest escaping through Valencia to Puerto Cabello. The battle lasted one hour.   One month later, 29 July, Bolívar entered Caracas, and all Venezuela except Puerto Cabello and Cumaná was then free of Spanish troops.

CARACAS.   In 1567 Diego de Losada founded a settlement which was called Santiago de León de Caracas.   It derived its wealth from cacao and tobacco plantations. It became the colonial capital in 1576, being politically subordinate in the colonial period first to Santo Domingo and then to Bogotá.   In 1595 it was sacked by the Englishman, Amyas Preston, and in 1766 it was raided by the French.   It was the birth place of Bolívar (1783) and of Francisco de Miranda (ca. 1750). Independence was proclaimed here in 1811.   There was an earthquake in 1812.   It became the capital of Venezuela in 1829.   The tenth Inter-American Conference was held here in 1954.

CARACAS COMPANY   see   COMPAÑIA GUIPUZCOANA.

CARACAS CONFERENCE. It was held in March, 1954 and
all the American republics except Costa Rica sent
delegates. Costa Rica declined because the host
country was ruled by a dictator. An anti-communist
declaration was approved 17-1, Guatemala dissenting
and Mexico and Argentina abstaining. The resolution
demanding complete elimination of European colonies
in the Americas was passed 19-0, the United States
abstaining.

CARACAS INDIANS. A warlike group, they developed a
strong, closely-knit order, combining hunting and
fishing with agriculture. They grew crops of cotton,
tobacco, sweet manioc, and maize. They also do-
mesticated wildlife, kept bees, and dried food. The
essential feature of their life was the political organization. There was a graded military class with the
rank indicated by tattooing. The subtribes had caci-
ques, forming together in times of war into a large
federation.

CARIB INDIANS. They flourished along the coast of the
Caribbean from Caracas to the Orinoco. The Caracas
were the most westerly of these tribes. East of the
Caracas tribes dwelled the Chaima, the Palenque, and
the Tumuza. Along the coast the Caribs were only
slightly more cannibalistic than their mountain rela-
tives.

CARILLO, CRUZ, 1786-1865. Falling prisoner in the disas-
ter of 1812, he was with Urdaneta in 1814 and with
Bolívar in 1818 in the campaign of Los Llanos and in
the battles of Calabozo and El Sombrero. He also
made the Boyacá campaign. He governed Trujillo on
and off during 1820-1822 and 1841-1845. He was a
Deputy to the Admirable Congress in 1830 and was
made General of Division in 1831. During the 1848
wars, he was with Páez.

CARTAGENA, MANIFESTO DE. In this manifesto, dated
15 December 1812, Simón Bolívar considered Venezuela's fall and the lesson it provided all of the South
American people. He appealed to the Colombians not
to follow the suspicions and errors of the Venezuelan
Republic and urged the necessity of freeing Venezuela.
The manifesto contained Bolívar's ideas on government.

CARVAJAL, JUAN DE. Arriving at Coro in January, 1545 as interim lieutenant to the Governor of Venezuela, he forged the credentials of the Governor and presented himself as the new Governor at Coro. He then decided to explore the interior. At the site of El Tocuyo he met Hutten who was on his way back to Coro in 1546. He captured Hutten and beheaded him. The murder caused the Welser lease to be revoked. The new Spanish Governor, Juan Pérez de Tolosa, hung Carvajal from his own gallows in El Tocuyo in 1547.

CASA LEON, MARQUES DE; or ANTONIO FERNANDEZ DE LEON. As a rich proprietor with vast tracts in the valley of Aragua, he served Francisco de Miranda, Monteverde, Simón Bolívar, Boves, and Morillo. As soon as one army began to desert Caracas, he quietly moved to the enemy, offering to help the victor. His lands grew and he prospered.

CASAÑAS, DR. SEBASTIAN. Minister of Interior and Exterior as well as governor, he fought against Guzmán. He was Deputy for Carabobo in the Congress of 1890.

CASAÑAS, JOSE ISIDORO. He was a merchant and farmer, and was once Minister of the Interior. He was a political brother to Ernesto Beauperthuy, President of the State of Bermúdez. He was Deputy for Bermúdez in the Congress of 1890.

CASANOVA, PASCUAL. Liberal Minister of Foreign Relations and enemy of Guzmán, he was afterwards a Deputy from Lara in the Congress of 1890. He had resigned as Minister of State to attend the Congress.

CASAS, BARTOLOME DE LAS, 1474-1566. A priest who was called "Apostle of the Indians," he made unsuccessful attempts in 1513 and 1518 to start monasteries on the Venezuelan coast. He advocated Negro slavery because he so loved the Indians. He advocated the importation of Negroes under the control of the crown and the distribution at cost of these Negroes to colonists who were willing to accept the obligation of converting them to Christianity. He was the first person to receive holy orders in America. In 1515 he was named to head a commission of priests to study the means of correcting abuses to the Indians. In

1520 he received permission to govern the area from eastern Venezuela to Santa Marta, Colombia. He wanted to civilize the Indians there, but he failed partly because of the previous scare by Ocampo and partly because his own leader in Venezuela, Francisco de Soto, terrified the Indians and enslaved them. He wrote the History of the Indies.

CASAS, DON JUAN DE LAS. When Ferdinand was made King in Spain in 1808, Las Casas was uncertain whether he should support France or England. Some imprudent acts rather than his indecision were the causes for his being replaced as Captain-General by Vicente Emparán. Las Casas had been Captain-General in Venezuela 9 October 1807-17 May 1809.

CASAS, MANUEL MARIA. As chief of the La Guaira port in 1812 he detained Miranda at the port on 30 July 1812. Miranda was jailed by the patriots on the morning of the 31st. Casas delivered him to the Spaniards. He put another embargo on La Guaira and then trapped 400 patriots.

CASTELLANOS, JUAN DE. He set down his impression in Elegías de varones ilustres de Indias. The work is often animated and colorful, incorporating classical history, literature, and imagination.

CASTELLON, JACOME. In 1523 he founded the fortified city of Nueva Córdoba which is known today as Cumaná. He massacred the Indians there.

CASTRO, CIPRIANO, c. 1858-1924. From exile, along with Juan Vicente Gómez, he entered Venezuela on 23 May 1899 and led the successful revolt against Ignacio Andrade. His forces won a decisive victory over the government forces at Tocuyito near Valencia and on 22 October 1899 he marched into Caracas. The "Supreme Military Leader" 1899-1902, he became Provisional President in 1899, but was opposed by regional caudillos for two years. Gómez vanquished the opposition, defeating Matos and the Liberating Revolution, 1901-1903. There was a new constitution in 1901. Castro, who was despotic, reckless, licentious, and corrupt, is known for the most corrupt and inefficient regime in Venezuela's history. He mistreated foreign diplomats and businessmen. The Second Venezuelan Incident occurred in 1902 when England, Germany, and Italy sent warships to blockade the Venezuelan ports in order to get the money which was owed to them by Venezuela. Venezuelan naval vessels were seized and German cruisers bombarded Puerto Cabello and Maracaibo. Roosevelt threatened to send warships. The Hague Tribunal declared that Venezuela had to reserve 30% of its customs receipts in order to pay the creditors, but Castro still defaulted on the loans and continued to mistreat the foreign representatives. In 1908 his health failed and Castro went to Europe for treatment. Within a month, Gómez who had been Vice-President, usurped the Presidency. Castro was exiled for life and Juan Vicente Gómez became dictator, ruling for twenty-seven years.

CASTRO, JUAN BAUTISTA, 1846-1915. Archbishop of Caracas and Venezuela in 1904, he founded El Ancor and was co-founder of La Religión.

CASTRO, JULIAN. The rebel army entered Caracas on 18 March 1858. A Conservative-Liberal coalition chose Castro as Provisional President, who had been the Governor of the Province of Carabobo. He persecuted the Liberals, causing Zamora and Falcón to go into exile after they had organized the Federal Movement. Tovar, Fermín Toro and Urrutia were in his first cabinet. There was a new constitution on 31 December 1858. In attempts to placate the Liberals he offered concessions which helped bring the country to civil war. Although the government forces were the Centralists, Castro secretly favored the Federalists. He was soon imprisoned by the government troops. By 1 August 1859 the Federalists had defeated the Centralist government troops and set up a provisional government. Tovar was declared President by the Conservatives and Castro was tried for treason. He was convicted, but was absolved.

CASTRO LEON, GENERAL. As a colonel, he was Minister of Defense, the only military minister in the cabinet appointed by the Junta of 1958. He was dismissed by Larrazábal in July 1958 when he demanded that the Communist influence in the government be lessened. A general strike was called and students demonstrated in support of the government, hoping thereby to pre-

vent a military takeover. The Armed Forces Staff
College closed, it having become a seat of anti-government agitation. All of the political parties, including the Communists, united to assure free elections and to prevent a military takeover. As a general, on 20 April 1960 he led the revolt in San Cristóbal, Táchira which was quickly put down. He was
imprisoned. Officers in the Valencia/Maracay area
were arrested for plotting to release him from the
Puerto Cabello prison and for plotting to overthrow
the government.

CEBALLOS, JOSE. A Spanish military leader at Coro in
    1812-1813, he was defeated by Bolívar at Carabobo on
    28 May 1814.

CEDEÑO, GREGORIO. As President of Carabobo he was de-
    nied the authority of constituent assembly and revolted
    in the name of Guzmán Blanco. He was rebelling
    against Gregorio Varela, the illegitimate brother of
    Alcántara, who was to succeed Alcántara. Cedeño
    thus helped prepare the way for Guzmán Blanco's re-
    turn to power in 1879 after the death of Linares
    Alcántara. Crespo and others soon joined him, call-
    ing the movement "Revindicating Revolution." After
    the battle of La Victoria, the armies united under
    Cedeño who entered Caracas. Guzmán Blanco was
    then declared the supreme dictator.

CEDEÑO, MANUEL, 1781-1821. Patriot leader in the Wars
    of Independence. He fought in the llanos and at the
    first battle of Carabobo. Piar was captured and ex-
    ecuted by him in 1817. One of the three members of
    Bolívar's Council of Government in 1818, he became
    the Governor of Guayana. He was with Bolívar at the
    second battle of Carabobo in 1821 and died while in
    the pursuit of the enemy afterwards.

CENTRAL HIGHLANDS. Composed of two ranges approxi-
    mately parallel to the coast, they are separated by an
    intermontane basin 30 miles wide in places. The in-
    land range has peaks over 4,000 feet and the coast
    range has peaks 5,000-8,000 feet. There are three
    valleys in the basin. Caracas at 3,000 feet com-
    pletely occupies one. There is also an extensive val-
    ley around Lake Valencia at 1,500 feet which is the
    most important agricultural area in the country.

CENTRALISTS. The government forces in the War of Federation, 1859-1863. They deposed President Castro and replaced him with Manuel Felipe de Tovar, the Vice-President, but Tovar did not wish to become dictator so he resigned in 1861. His successor, Vice-President Gual, was overthrown on 29 August 1861 and José Antonio Páez, who had been brought back by Pedro José Rojas, became dictator. Páez and Rojas robbed the Centralist government of its legal justifications so the army officers then deserted to the Federalists. In 1863 Páez made peace.

CEVALLOS, JOSE. In 1813 as Governor at Coro, he defeated the patriot army near Barquisimeto and then joined with the Royalist army that came from the llanos in December. He was defeated by Bolívar at Araure.

CHAKE INDIANS. Semi-nomadic and semi-agricultural, they lived in the general area from the Catatumbo River to the Río Negro in the Maracaibo Lake Basin. They were part of the community that were called Motilone (cut hair). They are still semi-nomadic, with a loose and ill-defined social order. They have a classless society whose life has changed little from that of pre-Colombian times.

CHICHIRIVICHI. In 1518 the Dominicans erected a monastery to the west of this locale. Alonso de Ojeda killed and enslaved some Indians nearby, and the Indians revenged themselves on the friars. When Ojeda returned to Chichirivichi he was ambushed and slain.

CHIRICOA. A group who lived on the llanos. They depended upon peccaries, deer, and other animals of the savannas as well as on wild plums and palm fruit.

CHIRINO, JOSE LEONARDO. A freed zambo (Indian-Negro halfbreed) who captained a slave insurrection at Coro in 1795 as a means of ending the white supremacy. He was defeated by the authorities when they were supported by the local creoles who were perturbed by such extremism. Chirino was hanged and quartered in Caracas.

CIRCULO DE BELLAS ARTES. A group who were led by Samys Mutznez in 1912. They painted the landscape

surrounding Caracas from nature instead of in the
studio.   The rigidity of form and the dark palette
found in neoclassicism disappeared from their work.

CIUDAD BOLIVAR.   Founded in 1764 and given the name of
San Tomás de la Nueva Guayana, this city was later
called Angostura in 1768.   Bolívar reorganized his
forces here after suffering defeat.   In 1819 the revolutionary congress met and proclaimed Bolívar as
President of the Republic of Venezuela and in December of that year as President of Gran Colombia.   In
1849 the name of the city was changed to Ciudad Bolívar.

CLEMENTE, LINO DE, 1767-1838.   In 1810 he was named
Secretary of War and Navy by the Patriotic Junta. He
was a representative to the Congress of 1811, and
achieved various military ranks and positions until his
retirement in 1830.

COAT OF ARMS.   The official coat of arms is a shield which
is surmounted by two horns of plenty that are linked
by a laurel branch which is flanked on the right by a
laurel branch and on the left by a palm branch.   The
upper half of the shield is divided into two square
fields.   The left section, colored red, has a bundle
of wheat stalks, symbolizing both the union and agricultural wealth.   In the right field, which is colored
yellow, there is a trophy of arms and national flags.
The lower half is a blue field on which is represented
a white horse running free, symbolizing liberty.   Con-
necting the flanking branches is a ribbon in national
colors bearing, to the left, the inscription "10 de
Abril de 1810--Independencia"; to the right, "1850--
Federación"; and in the center, "República de Venezuela. "

COCHE, TREATY OF.   In 1863 Antonio Guzmán Blanco met
with Pedro José Rojas, the government minister, at
a hacienda called Coche, just outside of Caracas.   The
Treaty of Coche provided for the termination of hostilities of the War of Federation and for the appoint-
ment of an assembly which would be partly chosen by
Páez and partly by Falcón.   The negotiators agreed
that Falcón would be the new President and that Páez
would leave the country.   The secret meeting was
completed by Guzmán Blanco and Rojas on 24 April

1863. It was ratified by Páez on 6 June 1863.

COLINA, GENERAL LEON. His activity dating from the
Brave War, he was Senator from Lara in the Congress of 1890. In the campaign against Matías Salazar he was defeated by Salazar at Tinaquillo.

COLL, PEDRO EMILIO. Essayist who was part of the
Cosmópolis group or the Generation of '95.

COLLADO, GOVERNOR. In 1559 at Valencia he made
Francisco Fajardo a lieutenant general and gave him
30 men to conquer the valleys that were inhabited by
the Caracas tribes. Fajardo founded San Francisco
and El Collado.

COLON FUENTES, CARLOS J. In 1858 the guerrilla units
that operated in Guárico, Portuguesa and Barinas proclaimed themselves Liberals and for the most part
joined together under the leadership of Colón Fuentes.

COMITE ORGANIZADOR PRO ELECCION INDEPENDIENTE.
Essentially a Christian-Socialist Party which draws
support from the church as well as from the moder-
ates among the professions. In 1936 Rafael Caldera
organized the Unión Nacional de Estudiantes which
split off from the Federación de Estudiantes de Venezuela. The leaders in 1936 were Caldera, Lorenzo
Fernández, Miguel Angel Landáez, and Victor Giménez
Landínez. Dissatisfied with the policies of the government in 1945, Caldera formed a new political party
in 1946, calling it Comité de Organización Política
Electoral Independiente. Others who joined him, be-
sides the 1936 group, were Edecio La Riva, Enrique
Acevedo Berti, and Pedro Pablo Aguilar. The party
gained 19 seats in the constitutional assembly election
of 1946. It opposed the government party in 1952 and
its leaders were imprisoned in 1953. The party's
name was later changed to Partido Social Cristiano,
but it is still known as COPEI. In the 1958 elections
the party was reorganized. Caldera represented it
unsuccessfully in the presidential elections of 1958
and 1963. In 1964 COPEI dropped from the coalition
with Acción Democrática. Caldera was elected President in the 1968 elections.

COMMITTEE FOR POLITICAL AND ELECTORAL ORGANIZA-

TION   see   COMITE ORGANIZADOR PRO ELECCION
INDEPENDIENTE.

COMMUNIST PARTY OF VENEZUELA   see   PARTIDO CO-
    MUNISTA VENEZOLANO

COMPAÑIA GUIPUZCOANA.   Formed in 1728 by the Spanish
    government for a trade monopoly with Venezuela, it
    was organized, staffed and financed principally by
    Basques who subsequently became unpopular.   The
    shareholders were the merchants of Guipuzcoa, the
    Spanish province of Guipuzcoa, the King of Spain, and
    some of the richest landowners of Caracas.   The of-
    fices were in San Sebastián until 1751 when they were
    moved to Madrid.   The contract was to send two
    armed ships annually to Venezuela, to clear the coasts
    of smugglers and the seas of pirates, and to stop the
    flow of contraband within the country.   The Governor
    of Caracas was the Judge Conservator of the Company
    in Venezuela.   In the War of Jenkin's Ear, 1739-1748,
    the Company helped to fight off the British attacks on
    Venezuela.   They also successfully eliminated the
    Dutch contraband in cacao and greatly contributed to
    the prosperity of the country by introducing cotton,
    indigo, and tobacco.   Although the Basques provided
    the trade outlets and thus insured a steady flow of
    goods from abroad, the Company paid badly and ex-
    tracted fat profits.   It sold goods to the colonists at
    higher prices than prevailed elsewhere in the Carib-
    bean.   In 1749 Juan Francisco León led a revolt.   In
    1751 a new governor threw the followers of León in
    jail, although a general amnesty had been declared
    previously.   León fought again and was captured in
    February, 1752.   He was sent to Spain where he was
    pardoned with the provision that he fight for Spain in
    Africa.   Conditions in the colony improved.   In 1777
    the restrictions on the importation of Negroes were
    abolished and the Intendency was established.   The In-
    tendency helped bring about the final dissolution of the
    Company by assuming many of its original functions.
    The War of 1779 was powerful in bringing about the
    end also, for Spain then granted the Venezuelans the
    right to trade with the Dutch and the French colonies.
    The contract of the Company was rescinded in 1781.
    The Company was liquidated in 1785 when its shares
    were bought up by the Royal Philippines Company, and
    the two firms merged.

CONFEDERACION DE TRABAJADORES DE AMERICA LATI-
NA. International confederation of unions, affiliated
with the Communist-controlled W. F. T. U.

CONFEDERACION DE TRABAJADORES DE VENEZUELA.
Dominant national labor organization which is composed of numerous labor federations: petroleum workers, construction workers, etc.

CONGRESS OF 1811. The first Venezuelan congress, beginning 2 March 1811, first at the house of the Count of
San Javier in Caracas and then in the Monastery of
San Francisco. It was composed of representatives
from Caracas, Barinas, Barcelona, Cumaná, Mérida,
and Trujillo. Confused, it spent four months sorting
out rules of procedure and working on minor issues.
The first President of the Congress was Dr. Felipe
Fermín Paúl; the Vice-President was Dr. Mariano de
la Cova; and the secretaries were Licentiates Miguel
José Sanz and Antonio Nicolás Briceño. The oath
that the deputies swore mentioned independence from
the Spanish government and representation residing in
the General Congress of Venezuela. The Junta resigned its power and the Congress elected an executive
body of three members who exchanged duties weekly.
On 28 March the executive body was: Cristóbal
Mendoza, Juan de Escalona, and Baltasar Pedrón;
with Manuel Moreno de Mendoza, Mauricio Ayala, and
Dr. Andrés Narvarte as substitutes. A High Court of
Justice and the commissions were created. Independence was declared on 5 July 1811, 44 deputies signing
the declaration. The first Venezuelan constitution,
which lasted three months, was created, approving a
federal form of government with seven autonomous
states. The national government under the constitution was charged with powers affecting only the mutual
interests of the constituent entities. By the time that
the constitutionally endowed Congress met in Valencia
on 16 March 1812 the Royalists had taken the offense.
The earthquake on 26 March 1812 had destroyed the
Republic and on 23 April 1812 the constitution was
scrapped, Francisco de Miranda being given unlimited
powers by Congress.

CONGRESS OF 1830. Convened at Valencia 6 May-14 October 1830. The delegates wrote a new constitution
which restricted suffrage to property owners. The

constitution reserved a measure of autonomy for the
provinces and municipalities.   Each province would
have its own legislature and its own governor to have
jurisdiction over purely local problems.   Freedom of
press, speech, and religion were guaranteed.   The
Conservatives upheld these principles in later years.
The Congress met again in March, 1831 in order to
proclaim Páez and Urbaneja as President and Vice-
President.

CONGRESS OF 1848.   Monagas' treachery infuriated the Congress.   At the meeting of 23 January 1848 the congressmen voted to examine the charges of infringement
of the constitution against Monagas.   Since they were
afraid of retaliation, the meeting was kept secret.
Monagas, however, was warned.   The next day a de-
tachment of government militia and a pro-Monagas
crowd appeared outside of the Congress.   In the fight
that ensued five deaths occurred.   When the congressmen heard the shots and shouts, they panicked.   Six
congressmen were then killed as they left the building.
Although it could not be proved that Monagas had di-
rected the assault on the Congress, he did celebrate
24 January as a national holiday.

LA CONJURA.   The period, 1906-1908, when Gómez was
knowingly being spied upon by men from Castro and
when he was subordinating every interest to maintain
his deception from Castro.

CONSERVATIVE PARTY.   A party of oligarchs, they upheld
the principles of the constitution of 1830.   In eighteen
years they amortized one-third of the national debt,
established foreign credit, negotiated a peace treaty
with Spain in 1845 and presented a legal government.
They threw support to José Tadeo Monagas in 1847,
who upon election dismissed the Conservative ministers.   The Conservative Congress was cowed by Monagas by his raid upon them.   The Conservatives and
Liberals joined forces to oust Monagas in 1858.   Julián
Castro became President after a thirteen day revolution.   There was another Conservative-Liberal coalition ten years later, in the 1868 Blue Revolution, but
the Liberals under Guzmán Blanco eventually gained
control of the country after the victory.   Guzmán
Blanco suppressed the Conservatives by terrorism
1870-1871.

CONSTITUTION OF 1811. The Congress of 1811 created the
        constitution on 21 December 1811. The provisions
        were for a three-man executive body elected for four
        years and a federal state to be called the Confedera-
        tion of the States of Venezuela. Each state was in-
        ternally independent. The legislature comprised a
        House of Representatives and a Senate, members of
        the former being elected for four years and members
        of the latter being elected for six years. The judicial
        power was in the Superior Court of Justice which was
        in the federal capital and in other lower courts. The
        clergy lost their fueros and the slave trade was abol-
        ished. Colored people were given equality with all
        others before the law.

CONSTITUTION OF 1819. The Constitution of 15 August 1819
        provided for a Senate whose members were chosen
        for life instead of Bolívar's proposed hereditary Sen-
        ate. The government was centralist with a president,
        elected for four years, who was responsible to the
        Senate. Each minister was responsible for his actions.
        The legislature was composed of the Senate and an
        elective Chamber of Representatives. The judicial
        body was independent, the judges being removable by
        impeachment.

CONSTITUTION OF 1830. This constitution, signed 22 Sep-
        tember and proclaimed 23 October 1830, declared the
        government to be republican, popular, representative,
        and responsible. It was an attempt to introduce a
        federal system. The electors and the elected officials
        could only be literate males over 21 years with either
        a small annual income from property or a larger sum
        that was derived by practicing a trade, profession, or
        office. The legislature was divided into a Senate and
        a House of Representatives, each province having two
        senators and representatives according to a formula
        based upon population. The President was elected for
        four years and was not eligible for immediate reelec-
        tion. The Vice-President was elected for four years
        in periods which overlap the last two years of one
        presidency and the first two years of the next. Both
        would be chosen by the Electoral College. Each of
        the thirteen provinces had a legislature and a governor.
        The governors would be nominated by the provincial
        deputation, but would be appointed by the President.
        A third level of government consisting of cantons and

municipalities was provided for. The justices of the
district courts and the supreme court were chosen for
four years and could be reappointed. The manumis-
sion age for slaves was raised to 21 years from 18
years.

CONSTITUTION OF 1857. Promulgated on 18 April 1857, the
constitution extended the presidential term to six
years and placed no restrictions on re-election. The
constitution was framed by José Tadeo Monagas and
was a cause for his overthrow in 1858. The President was given the freedom to choose the governors
of the provinces, and Congress was given the power
to choose the President and Vice-President for the
next term.

CONSTITUTION OF 1858. Promulgated on 31 December 1858,
it declared that the people exercise sovereignty directly through elections and indirectly through the authorities of the state. It provided for a carefully organized local governmental system which allowed the
provinces and districts to have a representative body
as well as an administrative structure. Direct elections were stated. Males were given universal suffrage. Federalism was accepted all but in name.

CONSTITUTION OF 1864. Passed on 28 March 1864 and put
into effect on 13 April 1864, the constitution incorporated the federalist principles for which the Liberals
had been fighting. Instead of local freedom, however,
the result was local tyranny during the period 1864-
1870. The country was named the United States of
Venezuela, the states being independent and united only
to form a nation. The President was elected by direct
and secret ballot for a four-year period and was not
eligible for immediate re-election. Twenty states
were made from the old provinces, each state to receive an annual subsidy which came mainly from customs duties. The municipal power was retained. The
legislature was composed of two chambers, a Senate
and a Chamber of Deputies. The judicial system was
coordinated so that the administration of justice within
each of the states was in agreement with the federal
judicial system. The internal affairs of each state
were proclaimed such that neither the federal government nor any other state could interfere with the internal affairs of any state.

CONSTITUTION OF 1872. Provided for democratic, repre-
    sentative government, for universal suffrage, and for
    the direct election of the President.

CONSTITUTION OF 1874. The constitution provided for pub-
    lic and signed ballots; for the responsibility of public
    servants for their actions; that there be no presiden-
    tially appointed substitutes in case of presidential ab-
    sence; for the reduction of the presidential term to
    two years; and that the President not be eligible for
    re-election and that his relatives not be eligible for
    election.

CONSTITUTION OF 1881. This constitution was called "La
    Suiza" because of the similarities to the Swiss Con-
    federation. Guzmán Blanco reduced the number of
    the states from 20 to nine and created a Consejo Fed-
    eral, composed of one senator and one deputy from
    each State, whose sole task was to elect the President
    of the Republic from amongst themselves.

CONSTITUTION OF 1901. Castro dictated a new constitution
    in order to give a semblance of legality to his rule.

CONSTITUTION OF 1936. The President's term was reduced
    from seven to five years. It prohibited the immediate
    re-election of the President. It was amended in April,
    1945 and was restored during the military junta that
    reigned in 1948.

CONSTITUTION OF 1945. The amended constitution of 1936
    provided for the direct election of the deputies to the
    Congress. The vote was given to women, and the
    judicial power was nationalized. It eliminated the
    part of the constitution that had outlawed communists.

CONSTITUTION OF 1947. The 22nd constitution, it became
    law on 5 July 1947, abrogating the Constitution of 1936
    as amended in April, 1945. There were guarantees
    of the right to work, organize, and strike, and re-
    ceive pensions, vacation pay, sick pay, severance pay,
    and a share in profits. The rights of private property
    were recognized and were guaranteed protection. The
    President was elected for four years by direct, uni-
    versal suffrage and could not be re-elected within
    eight years. There was a bicameral Congress which
    was elected by direct vote. There was a supreme

court.   The President still had the power to appoint
state governors and he was also authorized to order
the preventative detention of persons who were believed to plan the overthrow of the government.   This
constitution was abolished during the military junta
that took over in 1948.

CONSTITUTION OF 1953.   The President was granted overwhelming authority to rule as he pleased.

CONSTITUTION OF 1961.   On 23 January 1961 the new constitution guaranteed individual, social, economic, and
political rights.

REAL CONSULADO DE CARACAS.   Established in Caracas
in 1793, its membership was distributed among ha-
cendados, comericantes and mercaderes, broadly in-
clusive of the legally white population.   It provided a
forum for the advancement of economic production and
of trade as well as a locale in which to sharpen the
conflict of interest between the Creole growers and
intellectuals and the peninsular merchants.   The Consulado did not survive the Independence.   An official
merchant's guild, it had a tribunal of three to hear
cases between merchants without the intervention of
lawyers.   Esteban Fernández de León was the President of the Consulado.

COPLE, BATTLE OF.   One of the two proper battles of the
War of Federation.   The government troops swept the
field at Coplé, although they did not destroy the enemy.   Falcón collected Sotillo's forces together with
his own and turned towards the llanos, but on 17 February 1860 he was overtaken by the constitutional
forces under Febres Cordero, from Valencia, and was
smashed at Coplé, losing his army in the dispersal.

CORDILLA DE MERIDA.   Northeastern spur of the Andes,
extending approximately 200 miles and constituting the
backbone of Venezuela.   It varies in width 8-40 miles.
The highest peak is Pico Bolívar which is 16,427 feet.
There are large areas of páramo or mountain grass-
lands.

CORDIPLAN   see   OFICINA CENTRAL DE COORDINACION
Y PLANIFICACION ECONOMICA Y SOCIAL DE LA
PRESIDENCIA.

CORDOBA, FRAY FRANCISCO DE. With Fray Juan Gracés, they were the first two missionaries to die in Venezuela. In 1513 a monastery was built near present day Cumaná. The friars won the friendship of the natives, but unfortunately a Spanish ship later took the Indian chief and his entourage captive and then sailed away. The two Franciscan brothers were taken in reprisal. They later perished because the Spanish would not bring the Indians back.

CORPORACION VENEZOLANA DE FOMENTO. As a governmental entity within the Ministry of Development, it is largely autonomous in operation and responsible for a wide range of planning and developmental projects that affect the whole economy, especially the diversification of industry. It is thus the chief governmental channel for all private capital coming into Venezuela and also the government's lending agency to industry and business. It supervises subsidiary operative governmental corporations such as Corporación Venezolana de Guayana, Corporación Venezolana de Hierro, and Corporación Venezolana de Petróleo.

CORPORACION VENEZOLANA DE GUAYANA. Agency created by the federal government to direct the developmental program of Ciudad Guayana. The administrators are appointed in Caracas and have no local party ties. Since 1964 the local administration of the Corporación Venezolana de Guayana has been expanded.

CORREA, LUIS. As a representative of Costumbrismo he presented a portrait of Caracas in the 1830-1840's.

CORTES CAMPOMANES. Spaniard who fought for the patriots and who followed Bolívar to Nueva Granada.

CORTES MADRIAGA, JOSE, 1780-1826. Canon of the Caracas Cathedral in 1810. On 19 April 1810 he claimed before the Caracas Cabildo that Emparán had been hiding the truth and he asked for Emparán's removal. The cabildo rejected Emparán; the crowd outside also rejected him. The revolution had begun. By August, 1812 the revolution was over, and Madriaga was being shipped to Spain in chains. He escaped from prison and returned in 1814 to Margarita. He left Venezuela for Kingston and eventually died in Nueva Granada.

COVA, DR. MARIANO DE LA.   Vice-President of the National Congress of 1811.

CRESPO, JOAQUIN, 1845-1898.   In 1858 he joined the Liberals in the War of Federation.   In 1877-1878 he was
Minister of War.   He was given the title in 1879 "He-
ro of Duty Done."   As a general he supported Guzmán
Blanco and served as figurehead President, 1884-1886.
His term was noted for the economic slump that was
produced by a drop in coffee production.   Trying for
the presidency again in 1888, he lost to Rojas Paúl.
Crespo was jailed after an unsuccessful revolutionary
attempt.   In 1889 he was elected as a Senator for
Miranda, but he did not serve.   In 1892 he led the
revolution that deposed President Andueza Palacio and
he set up a dictatorship, 1892-1894.   After the new
Constitution of 1893, he was elected President, serving 1894-1898.   Although it was relatively quiet during
this period, his administration is noted for the sensa-
tional controversy between Venezuela and British
Guiana because of the gold discovery.   This event has
been called "The First Venezuelan Incident."   In the
arbitration Venezuela lost territory.   Crespo was
killed in the first battle with El Mocho Hernández
while attempting to defend the administration of his
successor, Ignacio Andrade.

CUBAGUA.   A settlement in 1500 in Nueva Esparta, it was
once famous for pearl fisheries and the site of the
ruins of Nueva Cádiz, the first Spanish settlement in
South America.   The inhuman conditions of work at
the slave camps here quickly exhausted the available
Indians whose life expectancy after arrival was said
to be one year.   After the pearl activity declined
about 1513, the Spanish turned to slavery.   The settlement was attacked by the Carib indians in 1515 and
in 1520.   It was destroyed in 1543 by a hurricane and
earthquakes.   By the end of the century nothing remained but stones and skeletons.

CUMANA.   Founded by Diego Castellón in 1523, it was first
known as Nueva Toledo.   It is the oldest existing
European-built settlement on the South American mainland.   It was important in colonial times as a center
of trade with Spain.   Captain Gonzalo de Ocampo had
laid the foundations of Nueva Toledo.   The settlement
was burned by Sir Walter Raleigh because the inhabit-

ants refused to supply him with provisions on his first
expedition to Venezuela.   Severe earthquakes wrecked
the town in 1766, 1797, and 1929.

CUMANAGOTO INDIANS.   A well-organized and warlike tribe
who fought against Garci-Gonzalez in 1579.   The smallpox epidemic of 1580 decimated the tribe.

-D-

DECLARATION OF THE RIGHTS OF MAN IN SOCIETY.   In
twenty-seven articles, this document was passed on
1 July 1811 along with the Declaration of the Rights
of the People.   Both documents preceded the Declaration of Independence which was signed on 5 July 1811.
Popular sovereignty, which was indispensable, inalien-
able, and indivisible, as well as liberty, security,
enjoyment of property, equality before the law, non-
perpetuity of public office, and happiness of all were
proclaimed as the aims of society.

DECLARATION OF THE RIGHTS OF THE PEOPLE.   This
document which was passed along with the Declaration
of the Rights of Man in Society on 1 July 1811 consisted of seven articles which give the duties of society to man.   Both documents preceded the Declaration
of Independence which was signed on 5 July 1811.

DECREE OF GUARANTEES.   Published by Falcón in August,
1863, it guaranteed the lives of all and abolished the
death penalty.   Property was guaranteed, as were the
inviolability of the home, the secrecy of one's papers
and correspondence, the freedom of thought and expression, and the right of universal suffrage for males,
of free association and petition, of liberty, of equality before the law, and of individual security.   The
decree abolished slavery forever and closed some
prisons.

DELGADO CHALBAUD, CARLOS.   His father having been
exiled by Gómez, he spent his youth in France.   He
was commissioned as captain by López Contreras.
He organized U. P. M. in 1945, and as a major was
selected to serve on the Acción Democrática junta in
1946.   He was the Defense Minister under both Betancourt and Gallegos.   In 1945-1948 he was unsuc-

cessful in smothering the antagonism between the
Táchira officers under Pérez Jiménez and Luís Felipe
Llovera Páez and the Acción Democrática government.
He led the coup that deposed the Gallegos government
in 1948.   Unlike the other two officers of the junta,
his attitude was of compromise and moderation.   He
was assassinated on 19 November 1950 by Rafael
Simón Urbina.

DELGADO CHALBAUD, GENERAL RAMON.   He was a
Castro supporter who switched to Gómez in 1908. Under the Gómez regime he was president of the government shipping company.   He thought of overthrowing
the government in 1913, but Gómez learned of the plot
and put him in prison for fourteen years.   On 11-12
August 1929 he was the leader of the invaders of Cumaná.   He died in the battle.

DEMOCRATIC NATIONAL PARTY see PARTIDO DEMOCRA-
TICA NACIONAL

DEMOCRATIC REPUBLICAN UNION   see   UNION REPUBLI-
CANA DEMOCRATICA

DIAZ RODRIGUEZ, MANUEL, 1868-1927.   Author and mas-
ter stylist, he wrote Sensaciones de viaje (1896),
Cuentos de color (1898), Idolos rotos (1907), and
Sangre Patricia.   The last two named books were set
in Caracas at the turn of the century.   They depicted
the artistic world of the aristocrat in conflict with
sordid realities.   In both, pessimistic protagonists
pursue a course of evasion in suicide or in exile.
The characters see themselves as superior individuals
who are above a society which can never understand
or appreciate them.

DIAZ SANCHEZ, RAMON, 1903- .   In Mene (1936) and in
Casandra (1957) he developed the social aspect of life
in the oilfields.   Barburata (1960) deals with the rise
of the urban middle class and the corresponding de-
cline of the landed aristocracy.

DIGEPOL   see   DIRECCION GENERAL DE POLICIAS.

DIRECCION GENERAL DE POLICIAS.   Under the Ministry of
Interior Relations, it is popularly referred to as the
political police.   Its major responsibilities are crime

prevention, anti-subversive measures, the supervision
of aliens, and narcotics control.

DISPENSAS DE COLOR. In the 18th Century the Crown began selling these color licenses which allowed the
purchasers to enjoy the prerogatives and status of
white men, regardless of their racial background. The
practice gave rise to the proverb, "El dinero blanqu-
ea, " money whitens the skin.

DOMINICAN ORDER. In 1518 the Dominicans established
themselves in a monastery at Chichirivichi. Two
years later Alonso de Ojeda preyed upon a tribe near
the Chichirivichi monastery, sailing away with 33
slaves. The Indians lopped off the heads of two
priests. Most of the friars were at Cubagua at the
time. When Ojeda returned to Chichirivichi, he was
slain. Earlier the Dominicans had been on the eastern coast in 1513, but the Indians had rebelled in 1515
and had destroyed the mission. By 1644 they were
established in the Barinas region.

DOMINICI, PEDRO CESAR. He developed the theme of exoticism in pre-Christian Alexandria in Dynonysos.

DRAGO DOCTRINE. During the controversy in 1902 between
Venezuela on the one hand and Britain, Italy and Germany on the other, Dr. Luís Drago, Minister of Foreign Relations, protested to the United States against
the use of force for the purpose of collecting debts.
He maintained that foreign debts could not be used as
an excuse by an European power for intervention in
any American nation, nor could they be collected by
force. A similar idea had been proposed 20 years
earlier by Carlos Calvo of Argentina. A modified
form of the Drago proposal was approved by the United
States at the Hague Convention (the Second Peace Conference) in 1907.

DUTCH NAVAL ASSAULT. In 1908 Castro dismissed the
minister from The Netherlands on charges of political
intrigue and stopped all trade between Venezuela and
the Dutch West Indies. A Dutch squadron appeared
off the coast, seized a port, and destroyed part of
Venezuela's navy.

-E-

EDUCATION, HISTORY OF. Simón Bolívar in the 16th Century was instrumental in establishing the first school
in Caracas, basically a seminary. An elementary
school at Caracas in 1567 was paid for by the town
council and by the citizens and another, private, one
was established in 1594. Chairs of grammar were
founded by Philip II in Caracas in 1593 and by Bishop
Alceaga in 1608. The monasteries supported both
primary and secondary schools in the large towns.
Philip II ordered the founding of a royal seminary in
1592, but it was 1673 before the Seminary of Santa
Rosa was established by Bishop Fray Antonio González
de Acuña. It became a university in 1721 and then became the Royal and Pontifical University of Caracas
in 1722. The Seminary of Mérida was founded in 1785
and in 1806 the Seminary granted degrees. Education
for everyone was originally included in the constitution
of Angostura in 1819. The Directorate of Public Education was established in 1839. Under Páez each
parish was supposed to have one grammar school.
There were to be colegios for secondary education in
the capital of each of the 13 provinces and the University of Caracas would provide the higher education
and professional training. During the 20 years of
Páez-Soublette, few schools were actually established
in the municipalities. Guzmán Blanco launched an effort to start universal education by equipping municipal
grammar schools and colegios. On 27 June 1870
Guzmán Blanco decreed that free obligatory primary
education for all children would be organized through
the National Directorate of Primary Education which
would be financed by a special national tax. The National Directorate was installed on 14 August 1870.
The Ministry of Education was established in 1881 and
the first Code of Education was adopted in 1897. López Contreras laid the basis for reforms in public education. In 1959 EDUPLAN, Oficina de Planeamiento
Integral de la Educación, was created.

EHINGER, AMBROSIO. First Governor of Venezuela, 1529-
1533. see ALFINGER, AMBROSIO.

EMAZABEL, DR. JOSE T. A President of the State of Bolívar and a Senator for Bolívar in the Congress of

1890.

EMPARAN, VICENTE. Former Governor of Cumaná who
replaced Don Juan de las Casas as Captain-General
on 17 May 1809. He ruled despotically and was dis-
liked by older men and by the church. He attacked
the prominent members of the colony for their revolutionary leanings, irritating thereby both the cabildo
and the Audiencia. In 1810 there was a frustrated attempt by the criollos (Creoles) to kidnap him. On 19
April 1810 he met with the Caracas cabildo in an attempt to dissuade them from forming a Venezuelan
junta. The cabildo, however, formed the Supreme
Junta for the Preservation of the Rights of Ferdinand
VII and even proposed that Emparán be president of
that body, although Emparán opposed its formation.
Cortés Madriaga, the Canon of the Caracas Cathedral,
persuaded the cabildo that Emparán had not been tell-
ing the truth to this body and Emparán was rejected
both by the members of the cabildo and by a crowd
outside of the building. A few days later Emparán
sailed to the United States and the revolution had begun.

ERNST, ADOLFO. German who came to Venezuela in 1861.
He became the Director of the National Museum and
the first professor of natural sciences at the Universidad Central. He challenged the traditionalists and the
theologians, introducing Darwin, Comte, and Spencer.

ESCALANTE, DIOGENES, 1879- . While he was Ambassador to the United States he agreed to become the candidate in 1945 for both the A. D. and the P. D. V. fac-
tions. When Escalante became ill two months before
the election, he was replaced by Angel Biaggini in the
Medina-controlled convention. Acción Democrática
withdrew its support from Medina and eventually took
over the government.

ESCALONA, JUAN DE. Along with Cristóbal Mendoza and
Baltasar Padrón, he was a member of the executive
body that was elected by the Congress on 28 March
1811. In 1824 there was a disagreement between
Escalona, who was then Intendant of the Department
of Venezuela, and General Páez concerning guerrilla
activity.

ESPAÑA, JOSE MARIA, 1761-1799. While Justice of Macuto,
     he organized with Manuel Gual the first armed con-
     spiracy against the Spanish rule. It was a rebellion
     of dissatisfied planters and army officers. The re-
     bellion in La Guaira was supported by Creoles, some
     coloreds, and by Picornell, Andrés, and Campomanes.
     By 8 May 1799 six of the top conspirators were
     hanged. Forty more were condemned to the dungeons
     in Puerto Rico and in Spain. España was beheaded
     and quartered. Gual was poisoned in 1800 by a fanat-
     ical Royalist.

ESPEJO, FRANCISCO. He was a member of the Patriotic
     Society in 1811 which was the center of political agita-
     tion. The Society attempted to pressure the Congress
     to declare complete independence. He was also a
     member of the provisional government of March, 1812
     along with Fernando Toro and Ustáriz.

ESTRADA, PEDRO. The National Security Chief in Pérez
     Jiménez's regime. After building a huge spy and po-
     lice organization, he was dismissed by Pérez Jiménez
     in 1958.

-F-

F. A. L. N.   see   FUERZAS ARMADAS DE LIBERACION NA-
     CIONAL.

F. C. V.   see   FEDERACION CAMPESINA DE VENEZUELA.

F. D. P.   see   FUERZA DEMOCRATICA POPULAR

F. E. I.   see   FRENTE ELECTORAL INDEPENDIENTE

F. L. N.   see   FRENTE DE LIBERACION NACIONAL

F. N. D.   see   FRENTE NACIONAL DEMOCRATICA

FAJARDO, FRANCISCO. Born on Margarita, he was the
     son of an Indian princess and a conquistador. In 1557
     he travelled with his mother, some indians and Euro-
     peans eastward to El Panecillo. They desired to
     found a colony called El Rosario. In a quarrel that
     ensued his mother and some colonists were killed.
     The Indian chief was hanged in reprisal and the set-

tlement abandoned.   In 1559 he travelled from the site
of El Rosario to Valencia where Governor Collado
made him a lieutenant general.   He travelled eastward
and founded an out-post which he called San Francisco,
near present-day Caracas, and a settlement which he
called El Collado, on the coast near present-day La
Guaira.   The Teques tribe rose under the leadership
of Guaicaipuro and the Spanish abandoned both San
Francisco and El Collado.   Fajardo was hanged in
Cumaná by a Spanish magistrate who feared his power.

FALCON, JUAN CRISOSTOMO, 1820-1870.   As a major, his
first revolutionary action occurred in 1848 against the
Monagas regime.   After the rebellion he served at
Maracaibo 1849-1853, returning to Coro in 1853 as a
colonel.   He was promoted in 1854 to general of division and in 1857 was given command of the Barquisimeto garrison.   With Ezequiel Zamora he organized
the Federalist invasion and persuaded Antonio Guzmán
Blanco to join the force in 1859.   Páez signed the
peace and Falcón became Provisional President on 17
June 1863.   In August, 1863 he signed the Decree of
Guarantees.   On 24 December 1863 he was elected
President by the Constituent Assembly, serving until
1868.   The new constitution established the principles
of federalism.   The name of the country was changed
to the United States of Venezuela.   During his four
years as President he was constantly putting down re-
volts.   As President he took little interest in government, being continually in Coro or away from Caracas.
He once proposed that whatever land he trod be declared the Federal District.   He was finally overthrown by José Tadeo Monagas and the Azules in 1868.
He went into exile and died 29 April 1870.

FALKE EXPEDITION.   Last large scale maneuver against
Gómez.   Under General Román Delgado Chalbaud 300
exiles sailed aboard the German vessel, Falke, to
battle the dictator.   They landed near Cumaná 11-12
August 1929.   The invasion lasted only a few hours
and Delgado Chalbaud was killed.

FARFAN BROTHERS.   Guerrilla leaders during Wars for
Independence who rebelled again in 1838.

FEDECAMARAS see FEDERACION DE CAMARAS DE CO-
MERCIO E INDUSTRIA

FEDERACION CAMPESINA DE VENEZUELA. The national
   peasants' union, by far the largest union in the country.

FEDERACION DE CAMARAS DE COMERCIO E INDUSTRIA.
   National Chamber of Commerce, corresponding roughly to the U.S. Chamber of Commerce.

FEDERACION DE ESTUDIANTES. In February, 1928 the
   Federación campaigned for the release of Jóvito
   Villalba and two other students who had been arrested.
   Two hundred other students were then jailed in Puerto
   Cabello and others began to protest against the government. Army officers then revolted on 7 April 1928
   but unsuccessfully. Members of this student group
   included Rómulo Betancourt, Germán Suárez Flamme-
   rich, Jóvito Villalba, Gerardo Sansón, and Luis Emilio
   Gómez Ruiz. On 14 February 1936 the Federación
   declared a general strike to protest the censorship
   board. When soldiers fired on the crowd, Villalba
   who was then head of the students, marched 30,000
   persons on the palace. López Contreras submitted
   to their demands by lifting the press ban and by charging Galavís with murder, removing most of the remaining Gomecistas from office. The Federación finally came apart because the members, drawn together by mutual hatred of Gómez went their separate political ways. The Catholics bolted when F.E.V. supported the education bill that secularized the religious
   schools. Others joined the Unión Nacional Republicana. The communists started the Partido Republicano Progresista. Betancourt founded Organización
   Venezolana.

FEDERAL WAR, 1859-1864. After the Monagas regime was
   overthrown in 1858, there was a bloody struggle of
   the local caudillos. The Federalists were opposed by
   conservative Centralists, the programs of each group
   being vague. During the first year of the war, the
   Federalists had two leaders, Ezequiel Zamora and
   Juan Crisóstomo Falcón. Zamora was killed at the
   battle of San Carlos. There were only two proper
   battles, Santa Inés, which was won by the Federalists,
   and Coplé, which was won by the Centralists. Neither
   battle was decisive however because there was no de-
   struction of the retreating armies. The Centralists
   were headed by Julián Castro, President of Venezuela,

who secretly favored the Federalists. He was replaced
by Manuel Felipe de Tovar, the Vice-President, who
then resigned because he did not wish to be a dictator.
In 1861 Pedro José Rojas brought Páez back to Venezuela. On 29 August 1861 Tovar's successor, Vice-
President Gual, was deposed and Páez became dictator. Loyal army officers then deserted to the Federalists. In 1863 Antonio Guzmán Blanco, who was
Falcón's Secretary General, met secretly with Pedro
José Rojas at a hacienda called Coche just outside of
Caracas and drew a treaty to end the war. The Federalist victory decentralized all future civil conflicts
among twenty centralized states. It was a climax of
a decade of increasing disorder in society. At the
end of the war almost all of the local governments
were headed by generals, some of whom could not
read or write. The war cost 40,000 lives and brought
economic ruin to the nation. Both Falcón and Guzmán
Blanco became the head of the government after the
war, Falcón immediately and Guzmán Blanco in 1870.

FEDERMANN, NICOLAS or NIKOLAUS, ca. 1501-1543. A
German explorer and adventurer, he set out in 1530
on an unauthorized expedition for El Dorado. As
Lieutenant Governor to Espira he reached the Colombian Andes in 1538. When he, Don Gonzalo Jiménez
de Quesada, and Sebastián de Benalcázar met in the
valley of Bogotá, the three decided to let Charles V
apportion the conquest. Federmann died before
Charles made up his mind.

FERNANDEZ, DR. EDMUNDO. One of the civilian members
of the Junta Revolucionaria in 1945. The Junta promised universal suffrage, direct election of the president, and a new constitution.

FERNANDEZ DE LEON, ANTONIO. One of forty-five Creoles
who petitioned Las Casas on 24 November 1808 for
the establishment of a junta which would be independent of Seville so that the political fate of Venezuela
could be decided. He was sent to Spain as a prisoner. In 1812 he was a Royalist.

FERNANDEZ DE LEON, ESTEBAN. Intendant of the Province of Caracas and President of the Consulado.
Along with his brother, Antonio, he was opposed to
the Captain-General and to the Basque element which

still sought to control the economic life of Venezuela after the termination of the Compañía Guipuzcoana.

FERNANDEZ DE SERPA, DIEGO. Led the expedition in 1569 that resulted in the founding of Nueva Córdoba.

FERNANDEZ VINONI, LIEUTENANT FRANCISCO. As a Republican officer on 30 June 1812 he changed sides and seized the fort of San Felipe. He trained the guns on Puerto Cabello, opening fire. The Royalist prisoners who had been held there were thus freed. By 6 July 1812 Bolívar had departed in defeat and Monteverde was arriving from Valencia.

FLAG. It is a tricolor of yellow, blue, and red horizontal stripes. In the center of the blue stripe there is an arc of seven white stars which represent the original seven states. In the yellow or upper stripe, next to the hoist, is the national coat of arms (which is omitted on the merchant flag). The tricolor was designed by Francisco de Miranda and was first flown by him on the Leander. The symbolism is the separation of Venezuela (which is represented by yellow, or gold) from Spain (which is represented by red) by the sea.

FLORES, JUAN JOSE, 1800-1864. A Royalist prisoner in 1814, he afterwards made the 1816-1818 campaigns with Páez. In 1819 he was with Bolívar in Nueva Granada. In 1821 he made the Coro Campaign and fought at Carabobo. His later military career was with Bolívar. He was elected as the first President of Ecuador in 1830. Although he did return to Venezuela for a short time in 1857, his later career was in Ecuador.

FLOWER. The national flower is a species of the white orchid that is called "Flor de Mayo" (Cattleya mossiae).

FONSECA, GENERAL RAIMUNDO. Candidate for President in 1888, he was a Liberal Deputy for Carabobo to the Congress of 1890.

FOREIGN CLAIMS AND INTERVENTIONS. The early national history is relatively free of foreign complications. The Conservative oligarchy honored all international obligations. The Liberal oligarchy in 1848 did not have the same attitude towards responsibility. The

United States in 1848 was asked by Venezuelan nationals to send its navy in order to protect U.S. lives and property. In 1849 the Venezuelan government declared a moratorium on payments of the London bank loans, whereupon Great Britain sent warships to La Guaira. In the same year Venezuela was forced to sign two claims conventions with the United States. In 1856 the Dutch fleet was sent to Venezuela in order to collect damages that were claimed by its citizens. In 1858 the British and French fleets blockaded La Guaira to force the release from the Venezuelan government of the deposed Monagas. In 1860 Spain issued an ultimatum to Venezuela to grant better protection to Spanish property and citizens. In the 1860's both France and Spain several times sent warships to exact claims for damages that resulted from the involvement of their nationals in the turmoil of this period. European warships appeared off the coast during the period of Guzmán Blanco because of default in payments of loans. Claims commissions eventually settled these matters. See also the first and second VENEZUELAN INCIDENTS.

FORTIQUE, ALEJO, 1797-1845. He was one of the most vocal of the separatists at the Assembly of 25 October 1829. He served as secretary of that assembly. He was also a member of the Congress of Valencia in 1830. Following the establishment of the government he was given diplomatic posts and was the Ambassador to London during the complications concerning the boundary disputes with British Guiana over the Schomburgk Line.

FOSSI, FRANCISCO. On the pretext that enemies in Curaçao were smuggling arms to Venezuela, Guzmán Blanco in 1874 closed the ports of Maracaibo and La Vela de Coro, awarding the navigation monopoly to Francisco Fossi and Antonio Aranguen, who were both his partners.

FRANCISCAN ORDER. The first missionaries who were killed in Venezuela were Fray Francisco de Córdoba and Fray Juan Garcés who had established a monastery near present-day Cumaná in 1513. In 1518 the Franciscans had reestablished themselves in that monastery, but the monastery was burned by the indians in 1520.

FRENTE CIVIL VENEZOLANO. In 1958 the leaders of A.D.,
U.R.D. and COPEI met in New York City and formed
this coalition, pledging to return a constitutional government to Venezuela. They could not agree on any
candidate for President.

FRENTE DE LIBERACION NACIONAL. The self-styled
movement of the Castro-communist opposition in the
1960's. It is not recognized as an entity by the government.

FRENTE ELECTORAL INDEPENDIENTE. Name of the party
that was formed by the junta in 1951. In the election
of 1952 a F.E.I. victory was proclaimed by Pérez
Jiménez who became the Provisional President when
the junta was dissolved. The Constituent Assembly
was under F.E.I. control in 1953 and elected Pérez
Jiménez as Constitutional President for five years,
beginning 16 April 1953.

FRENTE NACIONAL DEMOCRATICA. It was organized in
1963 as Independientes Pro-Frente Nacional to support
Arturo Uslar Pietri. The name was changed shortly
after the elections on 25 February 1964. A subsequent
decision to join a coalition with A.D. and U.R.D.
caused severe criticism for Uslar Pietri. In 1966 the
party withdrew from the government and joined the opposition.

FUENMAYOR, JUAN BAUTISTA, 1905- . One of the two
principal leaders of the Venezuelan Communist Party.
He withdrew from U.P. and formed the P.C.U. which
became known as the red communists.

FUERO. A body of privileges, rights, jurisdictions, functions, and obligations that was accorded by the Crown
to a town, corporation, association, class, or individual by charter or by law. There were more than
thirty types of fueros. The fuero was first abolished
for all in Venezuela in the Constitution of 1811.

FUERZA DEMOCRATICA POPULAR. Founded in 1963 by
Jorge Dáger, an ex-A.D. and ex-M.I.R. member, he
was preparing support for Wolfgang Larrazábal.
F.D.P. proposed a radical program. Larrazábal was
the only candidate for President to use imperialism
as a major issue.

FUERZAS ARMADAS DE COOPERACION.   Official title of the
    forces who are popularly and universally called the
    Guardia Nacional.   It is the branch of the armed
    forces that is responsible for public order and safety.

FUERZAS ARMADAS DE LIBERACION NACIONAL.   Com-
    posed at first of M. I. R. and P. C. V. members, this
    group conducted anti-government guerrilla warfare in
    the 1960's.   After 1966 it was composed only of hard-
    line miristas (members of M. I. R.).   The group had
    the blessing of Gustavo Machado and of Fidel Castro
    of Cuba.

                            -G-

GABALDON, J. R.   Although the revolt he led against Gómez
    in 1928 was welcomed in the foreign newspapers, it
    was crushed.   Gómez sent five generals to stamp out
    the movement which Gabaldón started in Lara, Tru-
    jillo and in Portuguesa in September, 1928.   Gabaldón
    was the Governor of Zamora and a man of honor, who
    resigned in protest against the brutality that was dis-
    played against the dissident students from the Univer-
    sity of Caracas.

LA GACETA DE CARACAS.   Established on 24 October 1808,
    it printed articles on issues such as monarchy versus
    republican government, religious tolerance and the
    freedom of worship, and the separation of church and
    state.   The newspaper continued until 1821.   Andrés
    Bello was an editor.

GALAVIS, FELIX.   Governor of the Federal District in 1936,
    he established the censorship board in February,
    1936.   On 14 February 1936 the Federación de Estu-
    diantes declared a strike to protest the censorship.
    Shots in the crowd wounded more than 200 persons and
    killed eight.   Jóvito Villalba then led the crowd to the
    presidential palace.   López Contreras, who had ap-
    pointed him in December, 1935, lifted the ban and
    charged Galavís with murder.

GALINDO, DR. FRANCISCO BAPTISTA.   A secretary of
    Gómez, he moderated some of the policies of the re-
    gime.   At one time he persuaded Gómez to release
    all of the political prisoners, to close the jails, and

to allow ten thousand exiles to return home.

GALLAGHER, MATTHEW. With James Lamb he brought the
first press from Trinidad in 1808.

GALLEGOS, MANUEL MODESTO. General, teacher, clerk,
trader, and politician. He joined Joaquín Crespo and
became a major in 1875. For four years he traveled
to and from Caracas and Puerto Cabello. In 1880 he
entered political office as a customs official. He later became Governor of the Federal Territory.

GALLEGOS, ROMULO, 1884- . He taught and administered
for many years in secondary schools. He was exiled
in Spain for five years of the Gómez era. Briefly
Minister of Education under López Contreras, he was
an unsuccessful candidate for President in 1941. As
a member of Acción Democrática he was elected President on 14 December 1947 and inaugurated on 15 February 1948 in the first genuinely free election. His
refusal of the demands by U. P. M. for a coalition government that would include COPEI was partly the reason that the military took over on 24 November 1948.
His books reflect a natural and human landscape with
the train of problems that beset Venezuelan society.
His first novel, El Ultimo solar (1920) has for its
theme the destructive natural environment and the social concerns that disturbed his generation. La Tre-
padora (1925) reflects the possibilities of new, con-
structive society. Doña Bárbara (1929) is a symbol
of the barbarism that must be destroyed before the
country can free the sleeping spirit of civilization.
Cantaclaro (1931) has the llanos as its setting, but in
a tranquil mood.

GARCES, FRAY JUAN. With Fray Francisco de Córdoba he
established in 1513 a monastery near present-day
Cumaná. When the Spanish ship captured the Indians
in slavery, the Indians retaliated and took the priests
captive. Months later they were killed by the Indians
because the Spanish never returned their captives.

GARCIA, DR. JOSE ROSARIO. Uncle of Juan Vicente Gómez,
being half-brother to his father, Pedro Cornelio Gómez. He was counselor to Gómez for many years.

GARCI-GONZALEZ DE SILVA. In the 1570's he established

the Spanish in the valley of Caracas. In 1578 he fought the Quiriquire and in 1579 the Cumanagoto effectively, weakening both tribes. He was characterized by his personal bravery, as exampled in his hand-to-hand combat with Chief Paramoconi.

GAZETA DE CARACAS. Established in 1808 as a newspaper in Caracas. See GACETA DE CARACAS.

GENERATION OF 1928. Refers back to the student strike of 1928 and the suppression by Gómez of the student members.

GIL FORTOUL, JOSE, 1861-1943. A writer, he methodically reconstructed the past in series of epochs rather than in events. In El Hombre y la historia (1896) he gave new importance to the society behind the heroes, bringing in the effects of economics, psychology, geography, and ethnics upon historical development. In Historia constitucional de Venezuela (1907) he traced the government to 1863. He was Minister of Public Instruction 1911-1912 and was President of the Senate in 1913. In the same year, 1913, Gómez faked an invasion and led the troops against the invaders, leaving the Presidency of the Republic to Gil Fortoul.

GOMEZ, JUAN VICENTE, 1859-1935. In 1892 he supported General María González who was commander of the government troops at Táchira. He lost a fortune and went into Colombia where he subsequently grew rich by rustling cattle. On 23 May 1899 he followed Cipriano Castro in the invasion of Táchira State. After Castro took over the government, Gómez became Governor of the Federal District. He then in 1900 became Governor of Táchira and was elected First Vice-President of Venezuela in February, 1901. He served as Vice-President and as commander of the army 1902-1908. When Castro 1906-1908 sent spies to Gómez's home, period of La Conjura, he restrained himself. Castro went to Europe in 1908 and Gómez seized the government, becoming dictator on 19 December 1908. Congress in 1909 passed a constitution which prohibited the re-election of the chief executive, but in 1913 the constitution was amended. Gómez was President-elect while Victorino Márquez Bustillos was Provisional President, and then was elected President in 1922. He resigned in 1929 and Congress

elected his choice as successor, Juan Bautista Pérez,
a Supreme Court Judge. Pérez served until 1931,
when Congress forced his resignation, electing Gómez
again. He eliminated regional, state, and local
caudillos by abolishing the militia and by building a
national army of career officers. He thus created
something similar to the oligarchic personalism of
colonial times. He ruled with an iron hand, often
treating his enemies with brutality. Yet censorship
and propaganda caused foreigners to believe that Venezuela was peaceful. He did restore the economic
prosperity and honored all reasonable claims against
the government. Foreign investors, including oil
prospectors, were welcomed. In fact an oil law was
drafted in 1918 which protected the national interests
and which was liberal to the oil companies. Gómez
overthrew the student revolution of 1928 and the invaders of Cumaná of 1929. He also suppressed the
attempt by General Rafael Simón Urbina in 1931.

GONZALEZ, JUAN VICENTE, 1808-1866. He exalted the
independence period, seeing it as the classical era of
Venezuelan history. Bolívar's "War to the Death"
pronouncement of 1814 was taken as the setting for
his first historical novel, Biografía de José Félix
Ribas. His Manual de historia universal was a colorful, passionate vision of history that communicated to
generations of school children. González became a
champion of the Conservatives, challenging Guzmán
and the Liberals in the 1840's.

GONZALEZ DE ACUÑA, BISHOP FRAY ANTONIO. A native
of Lima, Perú, he established in 1673 the Seminary
of Santa Rosa in Caracas, staffed by Venezuelans.
Eventually it became the University of Caracas.

GRAN COLOMBIA. The name given to the state which comprised Nueva Granada, Venezuela, and the Presidency
of Quito, its existence was proclaimed by the revolutionary Congress of Angostura in December, 1819.
In Spring, 1821 delegates from Venezuela and Colombia met at Cúcuta to arrange a formal joining of nations. The Cúcuta Congress proclaimed again the
new Republic of Gran Colombia. A constitution was
framed, the capital was fixed at Bogotá, and a provi-
sion was made to add Ecuador when the area was
freed. Bolívar was elected President and Francisco

de Paula Santander was Vice-President. Soon the
country was torn by dissensions and separatist move-
ments. By 1826 the Venezuelans under Páez had assumed a position of autonomy, no longer complying
with orders from Bogotá. In 1828 Bolívar called a
constitutional convention at Ocaña, Colombia, but the
convention broke up. In August, 1828 Bolívar became
dictator. The Venezuelan delegates did not even attend the constitutional convention in Bogotá in January,
1830. Instead Páez convoked a special constitutional
convention in Valencia. Venezuela thus withdrew in
1830 and Ecuador withdrew soon afterwards.

GRANDES CACAOS. In the 17th Century, the city Creoles,
owners of large estates which they seldom visited,
were called thus by the lower classes.

GUAHIBO. Indian group that lived on the llanos. They depended upon peccaries, deer and other animals of the
savannas, and on wild plums and palm fruit. They
were the most primitive tribes in Venezuela, being
nomadic and lacking in any social organization. The
political structure was a band of seven or eight families who were headed by a chief. Many such bands
moved in a tribal unit.

GUAICAIPURO. Chief of the Teques. He banded together a
confederation of the Caracas, Teques, and related
tribes to form a force of 10,000 who forced the aban-
donment of Nuestra Señora de Caraballeda and San
Francisco soon after their founding in 1562. Eventually he was killed along with his wife by the Spaniard,
Francisco Infante, who served under Diego de Losada.

GUAJIRO. Name comes from the semi-arid Guajira Peninsula. The Indians have a distinctive social structure
that is organized around a series of matrilineal, clan-
like groups. They live in temporary villages and are
cattle raisers, traders, and smugglers. Arawak-
speaking, they do much trading in milk and meat.
For them wealth is a source of power and status.
Hence they are the richest of the aborigines.

GUAL, MANUEL, 1749-1800 see JOSE MARIA ESPAÑA

GUAL, PEDRO, 1783-1862. A patriot, he was with Bolívar
in Nueva Granada. He became one of the important

civilians of the Republic of Gran Colombia. He was
the Civil Governor of Cartagena, a member of the
Congress of Cúcuta, Minister of the Treasury, and
best known as the Minister of Foreign Relations. He
drew up the program for the Congress of Panama and
left Colombian service in 1830, becoming an Ecudori-
an minister in Spain. He returned to Caracas in
1849, later being a member of the government that
was established at the fall of Julián Castro. In fact
he served as President from August to September,
1859. When Tovar became the constitutional President in April, 1860, Gual became Vice-President. He
became President in May, 1861 when Tovar resigned.
Gual asked Páez to resign as Minister of War and
Navy after he discovered Páez was attempting to ne-
gotiate with the Federalists. Gual was then arrested
in August, 1861 and Páez was proclaimed dictator.

GUERRA, CRISTOBAL. With his brother Luis and with
Pedro Alonso Niño in the second half of 1499, less
than a year after Columbus had left the Venezuelan
coast, he discovered the pearl beds near Margarita
and the Cubagua Islands. They explored the coast
and returned to Spain with a fortune. They were then
jailed by King Ferdinand on charges of hiding part of
the fortune in order to avoid sharing with the King.
They were released, however, when nothing could be
proven.

GUERRA, RAMON, 1843-?. In 1864 he served as majordomo
to a rancher, taking part in the Blue Revolution of
1868. He was opposed to the policies of Guzmán
Blanco and moved to Apure in 1872. He helped to defeat the Salazar rebellion. In 1879 he assisted the
return of Guzmán Blanco and in 1881 he was recalled
again to suppress the guerrilla groups. He was imprisoned in 1882, but released in 1886 because of ill
health. Finding his properties in ruin, he rebuilt his
fortune by 1892, joining Crespo's forces that year.
He served in the Crespo administration in the Constitutional Assembly, as Minister of War and Navy, and
as a member of the Grand Military Council. He defeated and imprisoned El Mocho Hernández for the
government. While provisional President of the State
of Guárico, he joined the 1899 Liberating Revolution
against the Andrade administration. He was defeated
in battle by government forces.

GUEVARA VASCONCELOS. Captain-General in 1800 who attempted to improve the administration of justice.

GUEVARA Y LIRA, SILVESTRE, 1814-1882. General José Gregorio Monagas as President of the Republic in 1852 elected Guevara y Lira as Archbishop of Caracas and Venezuela. The two major events during his reign as archbishop were the Concorde with the Holy See in 1862 and the conflict with the government of President Guzmán Blanco in September, 1870. Guevara y Lira resigned his archbishopric in May, 1876.

GUIANA HIGHLANDS. Almost immediately south of the lower Orinoco, the highlands cover almost half of the nation. It is a high plateau 1,500-3,000 feet above sea level. Some of the highest waterfalls in the world occur here, producing an unlimited source of water power. Some of the area is badly eroded; most has savanna grass and deciduous tropical forest. The highest peak, Mount Roraima at 9,219 feet, marks the junction of Venezuela, Brazil, and British Guiana. The tropical rain forest is in the southwestern part of the highlands.

GUTIERREZ COLL, JACINTO, 1835-1901. Minister of Foreign Relations in 1864 and 1870, ambassador to several European nations in 1865, and Venezuelan Consul General in New York in 1875, he is best known as one of the more inspired Venezuelan poets. Among his poems are "Nocturno," "La Vuelta a la Patria," "Caléndulas," "Soledad," "Las Golondrinas," and the sonnets called "Hojas."

GUZMAN, ANTONIO LEOCADIO, 1801-1884. When he returned to Venezuela in 1823 he started a newspaper called El Argos. He was Minister of Interior and Justice in 1830 and served Páez until 1839, being removed from the administration because of intrigues. In 1840 the Liberal Party established El Venezolano. Guzmán was its editor. From its pages he advocated universal suffrage, immediate emancipation of the slaves, and abolition of capital punishment for political crimes. He was exiled by Monagas, but was brought back in 1849 as Minister of Interior and Vice-President. In 1851 he was an unsuccessful candidate for President, being defeated by José Gregorio Monagas. In 1852 he was Ambassador to Perú. He was

a member of the Junta Patriótica de Venezuela in
Santo Tomás in 1858 prior to his joining Ezequiel
Zamora against the Castro government. In 1881 he
was the Venezuelan representative during the dispute
over the Venezuelan-Colombian border.

GUZMAN BLANCO, ANTONIO, 1829-1899. During the Monagas regime he was Consul in Philadelphia and New
York and was secretary of the Venezuelan embassy
in Washington. Losing his position in 1848 he returned to Venezuela. He was persuaded by General
Falcón in Curaçao to join his forces which invaded
Venezuela in 1859. With the rank of major and as
secretary to Falcón, he became editor of the army
newspaper. He was with Zamora when the latter died
at the battle of San Carlos. In 1863 Guzmán Blanco
met with Pedro José Rojas at Coche, outside of Caracas, and drafted the peace treaty. Serving as Vice-
President to Falcón, 1863-1868, he succeeded in
floating loans in Europe. He returned to Caracas after the death of Monagas in 1868. Leading the Forces
of Regeneration, Los Amarillos, he took Caracas on
27 April 1870. He dominated politics for the next
eighteen years. His first term as President, 1870-
1877, was called "El Septenio." He chose General
Linares Alcántara to succeed him as President in
1877 while he became a minister once more in Europe. When General Cedeño rebelled against the government in 1879, Guzmán Blanco returned and became
President, 1879-1884. This term was called "El
Quinquenio." He returned to Europe again during the
Crespo administration, 1884-1886. His last term as
President, 1886-1888, has been called "El Aclamación" or "El Bienio." He supported Rojas Paúl in
1888 and returned to Europe. Guzmán Blanco was an
able administrator who built roads, had the ports improved, constructed railroads, modernized cities,
provided for free and compulsory public education,
refunded the national debt, restored the national credit, and modernized the penal system. There were
two new constitutions, in 1874 and in 1881. The
presidential office was limited to two years, but the
President was chosen by the Federal Council. Guzmán
Blanco destroyed the remaining power of the church,
exiling the archbishop and abolishing ecclesiastical
privileges.

-H-

HAWKINS, JOHN. English pirate who in 1565 sailed into
    Borburata harbor with cargoes of Negroes, cloth, and
    wine. Governor Alonso Bernáldez permitted him to
    trade. Spain later fined Bernáldez for disregarding
    laws prohibiting trading with the British.

HERNANDEZ, JOSE MARIA. Called "El Mocho." In 1887
    he returned to Venezuela after wandering in the is-
    lands of the Antilles. He became a gold miner in
    Yuruay, entering local politics. He led a rebellion
    to unseat a territorial chief. In 1892 he took over
    the State of Bolívar. He subsequently visited the
    United States, but became involved in a lawsuit re-
    sulting from his cancellation of a contract while he
    was the President of the State of Bolívar. An unsuc-
    cessful candidate for President in 1897, as candidate
    for the Nationalist Party, he left Caracas in 1898 to
    begin a rebellion against the new administration of
    Andrade, who defeated him in the election. He con-
    tacted General Evaristo Lima, setting the date for 2
    March 1898. When news of the revolution got out,
    the uprising was advanced one day. During a battle,
    his forces killed Crespo. Hernández in turn was de-
    feated and jailed by General Ramón Guerra, but he
    was later released by Castro in 1899. He returned
    from exile in 1908 and was given a post by Gómez.

HERRERA, JOAQUIN. Liberal who joined forces with
    Wenceslao Urrutia to oust Monagas in 1858. Along
    with Manuel Felipe de Tovar and Fermín Toro, he
    chose Julián Castro, the Governor of Carabobo, to
    lead the Conservative revolution.

HOHERMUT, GEORGE see SPIRA, JORGE

HUMBOLDT, ALEXANDER VON. Prussian scientist who
    visited Venezuela as well as other Latin American
    countries, describing the people, public life, history,
    and geography during the first decades of the 19th
    Century.

HUTTEN, FELIPE DE. As lieutenant to Rodrigo de Basti-
    das, who was Governor, he departed from Coro in
    1541 to search for El Dorado. He fought a large

battle at Los Omeguas.   As he was returning in 1546
he met Juan Carvajal at El Tocuyo.   Carvajal took
Hutten prisoner and had him beheaded.

-I-

I. A. N.   see   INSTITUTO AGRARIO NACIONAL

I. N. C. E.   see   INSTITUTO NACIONAL DE COOPERACION
    EDUCATIVA

INDEPENDENCE, ACT OF.   Written by Roscio and Iznardi,
    it was approved by Congress on 5 July 1811, pub-
    lished on 14 July, and printed in the Gaceta de Cara-
    cas on 16 July.   The new country took the name of
    American Confederation of Venezuela.   It comprised
    the provinces of Caracas, Cumaná, Barinas, Marga-
    rita, Barcelona, Mérida, and Trujillo.   The Manifesto
    to the World on 30 July 1811 gave the reasons for the
    declaration of independence.

INDEPENDENCE DAY.   5 July 1811.   Although some mem-
    bers of Congress wished to declare independence on
    4 July to coincide with the United States' independence
    day, the vote was not taken until the 5th.   38 of 44
    deputies signed the declaration.   Venezuela then be-
    came a confederation of free, sovereign, and inde-
    pendent states.   The argument for independence was
    based on Ferdinand's transfer of his powers and sub-
    jects to Napoleon at Bayonne.   It was claimed that
    Ferdinand had thus forfeited the right to rule over
    free men.   The statement was preceded on 1 July
    1811 by the Declaration of the Rights of the People
    and the Declaration of the Rights of Man in Society.

INDEPENDENT ELECTORAL FRONT   see   FRENTE
    ELECTORAL INDEPENDIENTE

INDIAN TRIBES.   In alphabetical order the following Indian
    tribes were important for Venezuelan history: Acha-
    gua, Arawak, Caberre, Caracas, Chaima, Chaké,
    Cumanagoto, Gandule, Guahibo, Guajiro, Guayupe,
    Jirajira, Maracapan, Mariche, Omegua, Otomac, Pa-
    lenque, Paria, Quiriquire, Sáliva, Teques, Timote,
    Tumuzu, and Zorca.

INSTITUTO AGRARIO NACIONAL. Quasi-autonomous, mixed (private and public) commission that is charged with the responsibility for land reform and settlement.

INSTITUTO DE MAJORAMIENTO PROFESIONAL DEL MAGISTERIO. Organized to combat the problem of the low quality of teachers, its regional offices train non-degreed teachers and improve teaching techniques.

INSTITUTO NACIONAL DE COOPERACION EDUCATIVA. Autonomous education unit within the Ministry of Education that offers technical training for unskilled labor. Since 1964 it has placed a heavy emphasis on providing occupational training for young people.

INTENDANCY. Established in 1777 specifically for the stimulation of agriculture, the Intendant had dictatorial powers over economic matters. The office assumed most of the original functions of the Compañía Guipuzcoana. The Intendant was independent of the Governor and had powers fixed by ordinance. He appointed administrators for each branch of revenue, set up the Accountancy-General and Treasury-General, and used the provincial governors as his delegates within their provinces. The first Intendant was Abalos.

INTER-AMERICAN CENTER OF RURAL EDUCATION AT RUBIO. The center was opened in 1954 through the cooperation of the Venezuelan government, the Organization of American States, and UNESCO. It provided specialization in courses of administration and supervision, programs and methods, rural sociology and community education, agricultural education, and in home economics and health education.

INTER-AMERICAN CONFERENCE, TENTH. Held at Caracas, 1954, the threat of communism and hemispheric economic problems were the major topics of discussion. Venezuela supported both the U.S. resolution condemning international communism and the Latin-American sponsored resolution calling for greater collective efforts to solve economic problems.

IZNARDI, FRANCISCO. With Roscio he wrote the Act of Independence in July, 1811. Along with Gabriel Ponte, Roscio, and Francisco Javier Ustáriz, he was

mainly responsible for the constitution of 1811. In
August, 1812 he was shipped to Spain for his part in
the revolt.

-J-

JESUITS.   Penetrating the Orinco area in 1576, they later
worked on the Casanare, Meta, and Orinoco Rivers.

JUNTA PATRIOTICA.   Name of the summer, 1957 coalition
of A. D., U. R. D., COPEI, and P. C. V. in opposition
to the dictatorship of Pérez Jiménez.   After the overthrow of the government in January, 1958, the coalition minus P. C. V. met in New York City and formed
the Frente Civil Venezolano.

JUNTA REVOLUCIONARIA.   In 1945 Acción Democrática attacked Diógenes Biaggini who was the candidate that
Medina Angarita was supporting for President.   A. D.
allied themselves with young army officers and took
over the government.   In October, 1945 A. D. was
called to form a new government.   At first the government called itself the Junta Revolucionaria.   It
was composed of seven civilians--Rómulo Betancourt,
Luis Beltrán Prieto Figuerosa, Gonzalo Barrios,
Raúl Leoni, Dr. Edmundo Fernández--and two officers, Captain Mario Vargas and Major Carlos Delgado Chalbaud.   The Junta promised universal suffrage,
direct election of the President, and a new constitution.   It created a special Tribunal of Civil and Administrative Responsibility which tried López Contreras, Medina Angarita, Uslar Pietri.   These three
along with other politicians were exiled.

JUNTA SUPREMA.   Established 19 April 1810 by the Caracas Cabildo, it attempted to remain faithful to the
imprisoned King of Spain, yet remaining independent
of any existing Spanish authority.   The Junta almost
made Vicente Emparán, the Captain-General, its
president, but Cortés Madriaga, canon of the Caracas
Cathedral, convinced the members of the junta that
Emparán was unfaithful to the Venezuelans.   The
junta strengthened its position at home and sent Colonel Simón Bolívar and Luis López Méndez, with
Andrés Bello as secretary, to London for guarantees
of protection.   The mission precipitated the return

of Miranda to Venezuela. The junta abdicated its
power to the first Venezuelan Congress of March,
1811.

-L-

LABOR LAWS. In 1917 there was little protection for the
workers, but the 1922 law covering the petroleum industry made the companies responsible for the health
and well-being of the employees. Hospitals for the
workers were to be provided for, and accident, dis-
ability, and death benefits were specified. On 23 July 1928 a law covering all employees incorporated
the provisions of the petroleum law as well as a nine-
hour work day, the right to form unions, and the establishment of arbitration of labor disputes by state
governors. In 1936 the unions were allowed to affili-
ate with foreign organizations. The employer's responsibilities were expanded to sanitary housing, medical care for the families of the employees, and educational facilities for the children. The 1945 law
provided for compulsory profit sharing. On 3 November 1947 the 1936 law was revised according to the
standards of the I.L.O. The provisions of the law
apply to all citizens and foreigners, but not to the
armed forces or to public employees. The scope of
the protection to agricultural workers was decreased.

LAMB, CHARLES. With Matthew Gallagher, he brought the
first press from Trinidad to Venezuela in 1808.

LANDAETA, JUAN. Also known for his religious compositions, he was the composer of "Gloria al Bravo
Pueblo" which became the national anthem.

LANDER, TOMAS. A newspaper editor, he was one of the
founders of the Liberal Party in 1840.

LARA, JACINTO, 1778-1859. Making the campaigns of 1813
in the east as well as the campaigns of Cundinamarca,
the llanos, Guayana, Apure, Casanare, and Nueva
Granada, he was also at the first battle of Carabobo
and then in the Peruvian campaigns. He was one of
the patriots who fought campaigns for independence in
almost all of the South American countries.

LARA, JACINTO. A polished general, who was an intellectual and proud of his name, he was President of the
state which carried his family name, a minister, and
a candidate for President of the Republic. He was
Senator for Los Andes in the Congress of 1890.

LARRAZABAL, FELIPE, 1818-1873. Musician and author,
he was the first biographer of Bolívar when his Vida
de Bolívar appeared in 1865. He interpreted Bolívar
as a superhuman, quasi-divine person. His musical
compositions were lyrical and exaggeratedly sentiment-
al. It is said that he was partly influential in causing
Monagas to free the slaves. He persuaded Matías
Salazar to rebel against Guzmán Blanco in the hope
that Salazar would make him his minister.

LARRAZABAL, WOLFGANG. Leader of the rebellion of 21
January 1958, he headed the junta that was formed.
The army, national security forces, police, and executive branch were all purged of Pérez Jiménez supporters. The junta dissolved the Congress, the state
legislatures, and the municipal councils. Censorship
of the press was lifted, political prisoners were
freed, exiles were invited to return, and the universities were reopened. To counteract the financial
deficit, the junta on 20 December 1958 decreed a
sharp increase in income taxes and raised the tax on
the oil industry. Larrazábal was a U.R.D. candidate
for President, being supported also by the communists,
but he was defeated by Betancourt in the elections of
7 December 1958. He then returned to naval service
as Vice Admiral and was assigned a diplomatic post
in Chile. He was also F.D.P. candidate for President in 1964 and 1968.

LAW FOR THE FORMATION AND RENEWAL OF THE
FORCES OF LAND AND SEA OF 24 JUNE 1919.
Formally closed the era of the militia. Although the
militia was not directly attacked or mentioned in the
law, its continuation was not provided for.

LAZO MARTI, FRANCISCO. A poet whose "Silva Criolla"
in 1901 was a nostalgic, symbolic eulogy to the llanos.

LEAGUE OF NATIONS. On 3 March 1920 Venezuela became
a member of the League of Nations. It was concerned
mainly with such topics as compulsory arbitration and

intellectual cooperation.   The ninth assembly elected
Venezuela to permanent membership to the Council
in 1928.   In July, 1938 Venezuela withdrew from the
League without saying why.   It was conjectured that
she was dissatisfied with the protection that was given
the small powers.

LEON, JUAN FRANCISCO.   In 1749 he led the revolt against
the Compañía Guipuzcoana.   As an assistant lieutenant
of the armed forces and as commission judge in Pana-
quire, he was replaced without reason by the Basques
connected with the company.   As he marched towards
Caracas in protest, he was joined by others with different complaints.   When the governor promised to
act, León withdrew.   A general amnesty was declared.
In 1751 a new governor ignored the amnesty and pro-
ceeded to throw the followers of León into jail.   León
was forced to fight, and surrendered in February,
1752.   He was shipped to Spain on a death sentence,
but was pardoned by the King upon the condition that
he fight in Africa for Spain.   The revolt did inspire
some effective reforms of the Company.

LEONI, RAUL, 1906-   .   He was president of the student
group, F. E. V. , in 1927-1928, being considered a
member of the Generation of 1928.   He was in exile
in Colombia, 1928-1936.   He was one of the signa-
tories of the plan to defeat Gómez in 1931 at Barranquilla, Colombia.   His election as a national deputy
was annulled by the federal court in 1936 and he went
into exile again, 1937-1938.   A member of the national executive committee of A. D. since 1942, he was
also the editor of its weekly newspaper.   In 1945 he
was one of the civilians on the Junta Revolucionaria,
and the Minister of Labor, 1945-1948.   He was
elected President on 1 December 1963 and took office
on 11 March 1964, serving until 1969.   During his
term he had three cabinets which were resultant from
the political maneuvering during the period.   COPEI
split from its coalition with A. D. in 1964 and F. N. D.
was eliminated from the cabinet of March, 1966.

LEVEL, GENERAL ANDRES AURELIO.   The principal author
of the first census of Venezuela, he published many
statistical studies.   He was the administrator of customs in Ciudad Bolívar and Deputy for Miranda in the
Congress of 1890.

LEVEL DE GODA, GENERAL LUIS. He lost his hand in the
    battle of Santa Inés. After Coplé he took refuge in
    Colombia with Falcón, Guzmán, Arismendi, and Au-
    reliano Alfonso. He served in the Liberal army under
    General Tomás Cipriano de Mosquera. He fought at
    Sobachoque in 1860 and at Bogotá. He broke with
    Guzmán Blanco because of the dictatorship. A mem-
    ber of the National Academy of History, he was a
    Senator for Bolívar in the Congress of 1890.

LIBERAL PARTY. Formed in 1840 by Tomás Lander,
    Francisco Rodríquez, Juan Bautista Mijares, Diego
    Bautista Urbaneja, and Manuel Felipe de Tovar, it
    published the newspaper El Venezolano with Antonio
    Leocadio Guzmán as its editor. Monagas used the
    Liberals to help rout the Conservatives in Congress
    in 1847-1848. The Liberals then joined with the Con-
    servatives to fight Monagas in 1858. Afterwards they
    formed a coalition government. The Liberals backed
    Guzmán Blanco in 1870 and the Gran Partido Liberal
    became the only political party in the country. Lib-
    eralism in Venezuela provided the outlet for provin-
    cial freedom and for a demogogic excuse for oppor-
    tunistic caudillos. There were two factions: one
    which wanted to make the government more democrat-
    ic, represented by Lander and other founders. The
    other faction just wanted power.

LA LIBERTADORA REVOLUTION. Manuel Matos with some
    disillusioned officials and caudillos planned this rev-
    olution. While the caudillos revolted in the interior,
    Matos raided the coast with his ship in 1901. The
    Venezuelan government protested to the British be-
    cause of the ship's registry. Britain requested that
    Venezuela reimburse British residents for the losses
    that were incurred during the civil wars. The rebel-
    lion lasted for two years, during which time the Sec-
    ond Venezuelan Incident occurred. Gómez battled the
    insurgents during the two years of the war and e-
    merged triumphant in six campaigns. By July, 1903
    the revolution was squelched.

LIMA, EVARISTO. A general, political figure, and hacenda-
    do, he was contacted by José Hernández and set the
    date for rebellion as 2 March 1898. His finca of
    Queipa was the headquarters for the rebellion. The
    uprising began a day early with only 45 men. By 2

March 200 men had formed. General Cipriano Castro
eventually rose to victory.

LINARES ALCANTARA, FRANCISCO, ?-1878. He had been
    caudillo of the region of Aragua for almost twenty
    years and had aided in uniting the Federal troops in
    1862. Guzmán Blanco chose him to be President in
    1877. His unexpected death in November, 1878 an-
    archized the country. Gregorio Varela, Linares
    Alcántara's illegitimate brother, was selected by the
    anti-Guzmán forces to succeed Linares Alcántara.
    Being called El Gran Demócrata, Linares Alcántara
    had received from Congress an award of 100,000 pe-
    sos for his 30 years of service to democracy. This
    award enabled him to found an estate for his heirs.
    It is interesting that on 2 March 1877, he dismissed
    the entire army, replacing them with an entirely new
    force.

LISCANO, JUAN. Writing in the folklore vein, he is often
    considered as one of the best poets in Venezuela of
    this century.

LLANEROS. People of the llanos, in southwestern Venezuela
    and eastern Colombia. They were lancers for both
    sides during the Wars of Independence and were known
    as excellent horsemen and good fighters.

LLANOS. Flat plains which are drained by the Orinoco Riv-
    er. The term particularly refers to the plain north
    of the Colombian border towards the junction of the
    Meta and Orinoco Rivers, and thence eastward north
    of the Orinoco. The area is approximately 600 miles
    long and 200 miles wide, being covered with savanna
    grasses and patches of scrub forest and palms. Cat-
    tle chiefly graze there. Access to the region depends
    upon the navigable tributaries of the Orinoco. Ciudad
    Bolívar, 200 miles up the Orinoco, is an important
    river port. In order to conserve some of the heavy
    rainfall, dams have been planned, the pilot one being
    built across the Guárico River in 1956.

LLOVERA PAEZ, LUIS FELIPE. A member of the Táchira
    group, he was a member of the junta on 24 November
    1948. He became Minister of Interior and was sent
    abroad when Pérez Jiménez took over the government.

LOEFLING, PETTER. Arriving at Cumaná on 11 April
1754, his purpose was to study the natural history of
the area. He worked there for six months and then
departed for Barcelona and the Misiones de Píritu at
the city of Guayana where he worked three months.
He then went to the Misión de Caroní and returned
afterwards to Guayana where he became ill in 1755.
He received orders to sail to Misión de Murecuri
where he became ill again with intermittent fever.
This Swedish naturalist, disciple of Linnaeus, died on
22 February 1756.

LONDON LOAN. After Falcón became President, Guzmán
Blanco succeeded with the help of Giacomo Servadio
in floating a bond issue of which less than 25% ever
reached Venezuela. The loan was £1,500,000 but the
face value was £900,000. The issuing company with-
held a 6% interest and a 2% amortization in order to
cover the payments that would be due the bond buyers
during the first year. One third of the bonds were
sold on the market and the remaining two thirds went
to Servadio and to Guzmán Blanco. Servadio bought
£500,000 worth of bonds for only £5,188. It is esti-
mated that Guzmán Blanco made a profit of £176,000.
The bonds eventually produced £368,000 of which Venezuela actually received about £200,000.

LOPEZ, GENERAL HERMOGENES. As the first member of
the Federal Council, he had control of the government
in 1887 when Guzmán Blanco went to France.

LOPEZ, NARCISCO, 1797-1851. He fought for the Patriots
and later changed to the Royalists. In Cuba, he organized a revolutionary group which was defeated.
Fleeing to the United States in 1849, he organized a
group of North Americans to fight in Cuba. He was
arrested and prosecuted in the United States, but a
conviction could not be obtained. When he returned
to Cuba, he was captured and executed.

LOPEZ CONTRERAS, ELEAZAR, 1883- . In 1899 he took
part in the revolutionary movement by General Cipriano
Castro and also took part in the pacification campaign
of 1900-1903. In 1914-1920 he was Director of War,
purchasing military supplies in Europe. The attempt
at revolution on 7 April 1928 was foiled by him. He
was Minister of War and Marine in 1931-1935, and

after Gómez's death he became Provisional President.
In April, 1936 Congress elected him as President of
the country.   He broke the 27-day strike in July,
1936 and the labor law was negated.   There was a
large oil workers' strike in December, 1936.   In
March 1937, 27 of the most active opposition were exiled.   A three-year program for material, social and
educational improvement was installed in July, 1938.
That same year a new oil law was enacted, but was
ignored by the oil companies.   López Contreras had
asked that the presidential term be shortened to five
years and he refused re-election in 1941.   He chose
General Isías Medina Angarita, his Minister of War,
to succeed him.   The government of López Contreras
followed four lines: the creation of a national ideology that was based on a veneration of Bolívar; an effort to bring peaceful transition to democracy; an establishment of freedom of the press and freedom for
the people; and legality of methods in public affairs.
He was an independent candidate for President in
1945, but was exiled after the revolution of 1945.

LOPEZ MENDEZ, LUIS.   With Simón Bolívar and Andrés
Bello he went to England in 1810 to get assurances
that Britain would protect the Junta Suprema from possible retaliations by Spain.

LOSADA, DIEGO, ca. 1520-1569.   A Spanish colonizer, he
founded Santiago de León de Caracas in 1567.   He
killed Guaicaipuro who had been plaguing the Spaniards,
and he defeated the Negro slaves who, upon their revolt from the San Felipe mines, had declared war on
Barquisimeto.

-M-

M. E. N. I.   see   MOVIMIENTO ELECTORAL NACIONAL
INDEPENDIENTE.

M. I. R.   see   MOVIMIENTO DE LA IZQUIERDA REVOLU-
CIONARIA

M. R. P.   see   MOVIMIENTO REPUBLICANO PROGRESISTA

MACHADO MORALES, GUSTAVO, 1898- .   Spending years
in prison or in exile during the regime of Gómez, he

was leader of U. P., the name in 1941 of the Communist Party. When schism occurred in the Communist
Party, the U. P. wing became known as the black
communists and the P. C. U. became known as the red
communists. He was the communist candidate for the
1947 elections. He was in prison, 1963-1968. When
he was released he began an attempt to form a new
party called Union for Progress.

MANOA. The vision of the hidden lake city whose gleaming
gold turrets rivalled the sun. The Achugua indians
told this story and caused the Spaniards to search for
this El Dorado, the city of Manoa which was the fabulous domain of King Paititi. Sir Walter Raleigh
came to the Orinoco in search of this kingdom.

MARACAIBO. Ambrosio Alfinger (Ehinger) set up a camp
called Maracaibo, but the site soon declined. Alonso
Pacheco Maldonando explored the area from El Tocuyo, conquering the Maracaibo region, and founded a
town of that name in 1569. In 1667 Maracaibo and
Gilbraltar were attacked by Dutch pirates. In 1669
the town was captured by Henry Morgan. A revolt
against Spain broke out in 1799, but it was easily suppressed. The discovery of oil in 1914 made Maracaibo important.

MARACAIBO LOWLANDS. Between two spurs of the eastern
Cordillera of the Andes, they were formed by a grad-
ual filling of the depression, the center of which is
Lake Maracaibo (now called Lake Urdenata). The
basin, 100 miles long and 75 miles wide, is hot and
humid. The southern end of the lake region had
heavy rainfall. The lake at the deepest point is 160
feet. The shores are flat and only slightly above sea
level. Connected to the Gulf of Venezuela by a nar-
row strait, the lake can be entered by ocean-going
vessels. The petroleum field is under the depression.

MARACAPANA INDIANS. Used to cut off the arms and legs
of a captured chieftain. After he died, they would
open his stomach and eat his intestines.

MARGARITA. Principal island in a group which constitutes
the State of Nueva Esparta. It is rocky, mountainous,
with little rainfall. It was sighted by Columbus on 15
August 1498. Visited by Alonso de Ojeda in 1499, its

pearl beds were discovered by Cristóbal Guerra and
Pedro Alonso Niño. Margarita became the source of
provisions for the people of Cubagua. In 1525 it was
made an independent province under Marcelo de Villalobos, but he died before taking possession and his
daughter, Aldonza, was confirmed in the governorship,
governing through lieutenants. In 1561 Lope de Aguirre
kidnaped the governor and terrorized the inhabitants
for months. In 1600 the governorship passed to the
Crown.

MARIÑO, SANTIAGO, 1788-1854. He was a patriot guerrilla
leader in the east in 1811-1812. He launched an invasion from Trinidad in 1813, conquering the eastern
part of Venezuela, but refused to cooperate with the
Caracas government, forming his own state. In 1814
he decided to aid Bolívar and the Second Republic.
He sailed with Bolívar for Cartagena at the demise of
the Second Republic on 8 September 1814. In 1817 he
organized a private congress at Cariaco so that he
and not Bolívar could be declared the supreme army
commander. His army was soon defeated in a campaign where he lost Cumaná and Barcelona. He was
a member of the Congress of 1819 and was elected as
Vice-President of Venezuela in the new state of Gran
Colombia after both Roscio and Azuola died. He
swore obedience to Páez in 1826 and in 1835 was a
candidate for President. In 1835 after being defeated
for the Presidency, he took over the command of the
country and organized a military rule, calling the
Popular Assembly which confirmed his action and rec-
ommended a national convention. Páez was then appointed Provisional President with Mariño as military
commander-in-chief. When Vargas called Páez for
help, he accepted and defeated the insurgency of Mariño. Vargas returned to the Presidency. Mariño
was again defeated for the Presidency in 1850.

MARQUEZ BUSTILLOS, VICTORINO. Provisional President,
1915-1922, during Gómez's administration while the
latter was President-Elect.

MARTINEZ, JOSE LEANDRO. When Guzmán Blanco attacked
Caracas in April, 1870, the Blues were waiting for
the army of General Martínez which never came. He
was Senator for Zamora in the Congress of 1890.

MATOS, MANUEL ANTONIO. Bank and Minister of Finance
    under President Andrade. One of the wealthiest men
    in Venezuela, he raided the coast in 1901 while the
    caudillos revolted in the interior. La Libertadora
    was over by July, 1903.

MEDINA, JOSE RAMON, 1921- . Most promising of the
    younger poets. His intimate lyrical verse deals with
    idealized love, human fraternity, and tranquil pure
    nature. Three of his best known works are: Vísperos
    de la aldea, 1945-1948 (1949), Como la vida (1954),
    and En la reciente orilla (1956).

MEDINA, GENERAL ROSENDO. With Dr. Santiago Briceño
    he organized a local revolution in 1878.

MEDINA ANGARITA, ISAIAS, 1897-1953. Chief of Staff,
    1936, and Minister of War and Navy under López
    Contreras, 1936-1941, he was elected President by
    the Congress in 1941. He was well-intentioned, hon-
    est, and wanted to institute democracy, but it proved
    difficult. During his administration the income tax
    and social security were approved, and he insisted
    upon the freedom of speech and press. The Civil
    Code of 1942 was passed. On 13 March 1943 a new
    oil law was passed, increasing the royalties and taxes
    from oil. Concessions were to be renewed for 40
    years. Venezuela declared war on the Axis in Febru-
    ary, 1945. The constitutional reform of 1945 caused
    the direct election of the Chamber of Deputies. The
    vote was given to women in municipal elections, the
    judicial power was nationalized, and the Agrarian
    Law was passed in 1945. Medina Angarita broke with
    the Táchira clique. He was overthrown by a coalition
    of the military and Acción Democrática in October
    1945 and was sent into exile.

MENDOZA, CRISTOBAL, 1772-1829. One of the three mem-
    bers of the Executive Body of 28 March 1811. He
    was a substitute in the new provisional government of
    March, 1812 which served until a new constitution
    was approved. After the disaster of 1814 he went to
    the Antilles, returning later to Venezuela to admin-
    ister governmental posts. In 1826 he became the
    Intendant of Venezuela.

MENDOZA, DANIEL, 1823-1867. Costumbrismo-ist. He

described Caracas through the eyes of a rude llanero, Palmarote, who pointed to the shortcomings of the capital and to the excesses of the young intellectual romantics who sought through literary idealism and exoticism an escape from the chaotic conditions of national life.

META RIVER. Among the early expeditions there arose the legend that great riches were to be found on this river. Diego de Ordaz, Governor of the area from the Orinoco westward, took possession of the land in 1531 and was taken prisoner and sent back to Spain, but he died on the journey. Jerónimo de Ortal and Antonio Sedeño both searched for the river and its riches.

MICHELENA, ARTURO, 1863-1898. Neoclassicist painter who was a follower of Tovar y Tovar.

MICHELENA, SANTOS, 1797-1848. Economist, many times treasury minister, and many times envoy to Colombia, he thought that the customs duties were the easiest and cheapest way to collect all revenue. He also believed that the ad valorem duty was the most equitable and most convenient tax for an agricultural country, that tariff laws needed revision, and that smuggling had to be stopped. He was Vice-President of the Republic in 1840, discharging the duties of the President during short periods of the latter's absence. As representative to Congress in 1848, he was killed during the assault on Congress on 24 January 1848.

MIJARES, JUAN BAUTISTA. One of the founders of the Liberal Party.

MIRANDA, FRANCISCO DE, 1750-1816. He served as a captain in the Spanish Army, 1781-1782, against England in Florida and in the Bahamas during the American Revolution. He was accused of smuggling in 1782 and declared guilty, fined, deprived of his commission, and banished to Oran; but he fled from Cuba to the United States. He tried to persuade Alexander Hamilton and Henry Knox to aid the revolution in the Spanish colonies. In 1792 he fought as a lieutenant general in the French revolutionary army and was unjustly accused of treason and imprisoned, 1792-1797. On 2 February 1806 he secretly organized an expedition which sailed from New York to Venezuela. He

was aided by Admiral Cochrane in the West Indies.
Coro was occupied in August by his forces, but by 13
August he was forced to withdraw. He retired to
England, but returned to Venezuela 12 December 1810,
becoming active in politics. The Junta made him a
lieutenant general and in July, 1811 he was made commander of the Republican troops. On 23 April 1812
he was made dictator. On 25 July 1812 he agreed to
lay down arms if the Spanish would spare the lives
and property of the Venezuelans, but the agreement
was violated. Bolívar, believing that Miranda had be-
trayed him, wished him out of the way, and Casas
handed Miranda over to the Royalists. He died in
Spain in prison on 14 July 1816.

MIYARES, FERNANDO. When the Venezuelans were declared
    rebels in 1810, the Regency appointed Miyares, the
    former Governor of Maracaibo, as Captain-General.
    He, however, was ignored by Monteverde who in ef-
    fect became the Royalist Governor of the country.

MONAGAS, JOSE GREGORIO, 1795-1858. During the Wars
    of Independence, he fought at the battles of Maturín,
    Cachipo, La Puerta, Bocachica, Carabobo, Aragua
    de Barcelona, and Urica. He took part in the Rev-
    olution of Reforms in 1835, and was mentioned as a
    candidate for President in 1846 and 1847. He became
    President in 1851, but his term was a period of ter-
    rible revolutions. His main historical renown is his
    signing on 24 March 1854 of the law to abolish slav-
    ery. The militia was also reorganized in 1854. In
    1858 he was put in prison and died in the dungeons
    of the Castle of San Carlos.

MONAGAS, JOSE RUPERTO. The son of José Tadeo Mona-
    gas, he was made President by the Congress and took
    office on 8 March 1869. He was soon faced by a
    ministerial crisis and an outbreak of factionalism.
    His reign ended when Guzmán Blanco entered Caracas
    on 27 April 1870.

MONAGAS, JOSE TADEO, 1784-1868. Llanero, Liberal
    leader, general, and statesman. He fought along with
    Bolívar in the Wars for Independence and rebelled
    against Páez in 1831, but was defeated. In 1847 he
    was elected to succeed Soublette as President. After
    the election he dismissed the Conservative ministers

and replaced them with Liberals. On 23 January
1848 Congress voted to examine a possible charge
against him of an infringement of the constitution.
The massacre of 24 January ended the power of Congress. In 1851 his brother was elected President,
but in 1855 José Tadeo Monagas was returned to the
Presidency, serving the second time until 1858. He
had revised the constitution in 1857 so that he could
be re-elected, but everyone revolted. Caracas was
taken on 18 March 1858 and Monagas took refuge in
the French embassy. Urrutia, the Foreign Minister,
signed his safe conduct, and French and British ships
saw that the protocol was obeyed. Returning to Venezuela in 1864, he led the Blues in 1868 and captured
Caracas. He was named President, but held power
only a few months until November, 1868 when he died.

MONTES, FELIX. In 1913, the last year of Gómez's first
term Arévalo González proposed the candidacy of
Montes for President. Gómez then faked an invasion,
declaring a state of emergency and led the army
against the rebels. The constitution was then amended,
and two years later Gómez was elected for another
seven years.

MONTEVERDE, DOMINGO. As a relatively unknown naval
captain on 16 March 1812, he led the Royalists into
Siquisique near Coro and six days later occupied Ca-
rora. The earthquake on 26 March 1812 shook the
country. Ignoring orders from the Audiencia he captured Barquisimeto 7 April without a shot and took
Valencia on 3 May. With the aid of Manuel María
Casas, he captured many of the rebel leaders, thus
breaking the compact with Miranda in July, 1812. He
allowed Bolívar to leave the country. In 1813 Monteverde fled to Puerto Cabello after the battle of Taguanes. With reinforcements he marched towards Caracas, but, having lost the battle of Bárbula on 30 September, he went back to Puerto Cabello. At Las
Trincheras on 3 October 1813 he relinquished his command, after he had been shot in the jaw. In early
1814 he embarked from the country. For his Royalist efforts he won the honorary title of El Pacificador.

MORALES, FRANCISCO TOMAS. Assistant to Boves, he
defeated Bolívar in 1814 at Aragua de Barcelona. He
caught and executed José Félix Ribas, who had de-

feated him on 12 February 1814 with only school-boys
and students.   He later was with Morillo in Colombia
and defeated Bolívar at Ocumare in 1816.   He fought
beside La Torre at Carabobo on 24 June 1821.

MORALES, MANUEL.   During the revolution by Pulgar in
1870, he fought at Carúpano.   He served as red Chief
of Operations of the sections of Cumaná and Maturín
during the revolution by Crespo in 1892.

MORENO DE MENDOZA, MANUEL.   A substitute of the Executive Body of the government which was elected by
the Congress on 28 March 1811.

MORGAN, HENRY.   In his raid on Maracaibo and the lake
region in 1669, he set a new record for massacre
and pillage.   There were eight days of terror.   When
the six ships under Alonso del Campo y Espinoza
blockaded the exit from Lake Maracaibo, Morgan within an hour routed the entire fleet.

MORILLO, PABLO.   After the Napoleonic Wars he sailed to
the New World, replacing Cajigal as Captain-General
in April, 1815.   On 12 July 1815 he sailed for an
invasion of Nueva Granada.   When he returned to Venezuela in January, 1817 Caracas and the west were
commanded by the Royalists and the east was in patriot control.   In 1819 Bolívar and Páez destroyed
Morillo's cavalry at Queseras del Medio.   In 1820 the
war was stalemated.   Morillo was then ordered to
seek a reconciliation with the Venezuelan rebels.   On
25 November 1820 he arranged a six-months' armi-
stice.   Morillo then met Bolívar for the first time.
When he returned to Venezuela, Morillo resigned and
returned to Spain.

MOTILONES.   The most feared of the Indians, they live in
the Sierra de Perijá and neighboring areas of Colombia.   They belong to distinct tribal groups of the
Chaké and Mape.

MOVIMIENTO DE IZQUIERDA REVOLUCIONARIA.   This
marxist youth movement was formed in 1960 when
Domingo Alberto Rangel separated from A.D.   With
P.C.R. it launched an anti-governmental guerrilla
campaign under the name of Fuerzas Armadas de
Liberación Nacional.   Its rights to operate openly were

suspended in 1962 and it was outlawed in 1963.   In
1965 the group broke away to integrate into the
P. R. I. N. party.   In 1966 M. I. R. dissolved altogether.
It was also called Movimiento Independiente Revolucionario.

MOVIMIENTO DEMOCRATICA INDEPENDIENTE.   Formed
in 1966 from groups which splintered from U. R. D.

MOVIMIENTO ELECTORAL NACIONAL INDEPENDIENTE.
Faction of U. R. D. which in 1963 broke away from
Jóvito Villalba in support of the candidacy of Vice-Ad-
miral Wolfgang Larrazábal.

MOVIMIENTO REPUBLICANO PROGRESISTA.   Founded by
Ramón Escovar Salóm who was in A. D. until the
1950's, it is a minority group that is supported by
some middleclass, bankers, and merchants.

MOXO, SALVADOR.   When Morillo went to Nueva Granada
on 12 June 1815, Moxó was left as interim Captain-
General of Venezuela.   One of his posts was president
of the commission that confiscated the property of the
patriots while at the same time raising forced loans
to support the Royalist cause.

MUNICIPIO.   The smallest unit of delineated territory and
government in Venezuela, it typically comprises a
city or large town with a somewhat extensive and usu-
ally rural surrounding area which contains smaller
villages or hamlets.   In some respects, it resembles
a township in the United States.

MUNOZ TEBAR, JESUS, 1847-1909.   Engineer, Minister of
Public Works, and Rector of the Universidad Central,
he was a Senator for the State of Bolívar in the Congress of 1890.   He was also a candidate for President
of the Republic in the same year.

-N-

NAVARTE, ANDRES.   Vice-President of the Republic, who
exercised the powers of the Presidency, 1836-1837.

NATIONALIST PARTY.   The party of the followers of El
Mocho Hernández.   The Andrade government placed

them in prison.

NIÑO, PEDRO ALONSO. With Cristóbal Guerra in 1499 he
   discovered the pearl beds near Margarita and Cubagua
   islands and returned to Spain with the fortune. They
   were jailed by Ferdinand upon the suspicion that they
   hid part of the fortune in order to avoid sharing it
   with the crown. They were freed.

NORTHEASTERN HIGHLANDS. They constitute the eastern
   portion of the coastal range, terminating on the Paria
   Peninsula. The highest peak is 8,514 feet, overlook-
   ing Cumaná. They are sandstone mountains with no
   extensive fertile valleys. At the eastern end, the
   area produces coffee, cacao, sugar cane, and tobacco.

NUEVA SEGOVIA. Founded in 1552, it was later to be called
   Barquisimeto. The explorers found the gold mines of
   San Felipe nearby, and eight years later the Los Teques mines were discovered. The Negro slaves who
   worked the mines at San Felipe revolted, declaring
   war on Barquisimeto. The rebellion was crushed by
   Diego de Losada. The Jirajira Indians then revolted,
   but they were not completely subdued until 1628.
   Aguirre's men caused his death here in 1561.

                              -O-

O. R. I. T. see ORGANIZACION REGIONAL INTERAMERI-
   CANA DE TRABAJADORES

O. R. V. E. see ORGANIZACION REVOLUCIONARIA VENE-
   ZOLANA ELECTORAL

OCAMPO, GARCIA DE. With Juan de Vergara, he was a
   partner of Alonso de Ojeda in the 1502 voyage to Venezuela. The partners quarreled and threw Ojeda into
   the brig in chains. When they arrived in Hispaniola,
   the judges and the King and Queen cleared Ojeda of
   the charges.

OCAMPO, GONZALO DE. He was considered to be one of
   the most efficient butchers of Indians. He ambushed
   the Indian chief who had engineered Ojeda's murder
   and decimated the rest of the tribe by hanging, im-
   paling, and slavery. He then laid the foundations of

Nuevo Toledo, the first attempt to found a city on the soil of the Venezuelan mainland. These foundations were near present-day Cumaná.

OFICINA CENTRAL DE COORDINACION Y PLANIFICACION ECONOMICA Y SOCIAL DE LA PRESIDENCIA. Created in 1959, it is responsible for the integration of all national economic and social planning, and for providing and renewing nation four-year plans.

OJEDA, ALONSO DE. ?-1515 or 1516. Member of Columbus' second expedition, he was the first European to explore all of the Caribbean coast of Venezuela. He set out from Spain in May, 1499 accompanied by Amerigo Vespucci and Juan de la Cosa. They saw the villages that were built on piles over the waters and were reminded of Venice. Thus they called the area Venezuela or little Venice. They sailed along the coast to the Gulf of Paria, observed the Orinoco, touched at Trinidad and Margarita, and visited Curaçao. On 9 August 1499 they arrived at the tip of the Paraguaná Peninsula and thence went into Lake Maracaibo. He took an Indian girl who was named Isabel. His second voyage in 1502 with Juan de Vergara and García de Ocampo ended in a quarrel and with Ojeda in chains. After being cleared of the charges, he made a third voyage in 1505. A voyage from Hispaniola in 1509 to what is now Colombia ended tragically. Ojeda died in 1515 or 1516 in Santo Domingo. Isabel died shortly afterwards on his tomb.

OJEDA, ALONSO DE. ?-1520. He was said by Las Casas to be the father of the other Ojeda. In 1520 he preyed on the tribes near the Chichirivichi monastery. He sailed away with slaves, and the friars at the monastery were beheaded in retaliation. When Ojeda returned to Chichirivichi, he was ambushed and slain.

O'LEARY, DANIEL FLORENCIO, 1800-1854. Member of the British troops of 1818 and secretary to Anzoátegui, he fought in Nueva Granda, and at the second battle of Carabobo. After 1821, he served Bolívar in Colombia and Perú.

ORDAZ, DIEGO DE. Explorer who followed the Orinoco, 1531-1532, to the point at which it meets the Meta.

ORGANIC DECREE OF 27 AUGUST 1828.   Under this rule
    Bolívar suppressed the municipal councils and reor-
    ganized the provinces.

ORGANIZACION REGIONAL INTERAMERICANA DE TRABA-
    JADORES.   Latin American regional federation of
    unions to which the C. T. V. adheres.   It is affiliated
    with the I. C. F. T. U., the free-world international
    trade union organization.

ORGANIZACION REVOLUCIONARIA VENEZOLANA ELECTO-
    RAL.   Formed in 1936 but outlawed by López Contre-
    ras, it regrouped in 1937 as the Partido Democrática
    Nacional.   The communist elements were expelled in
    1937 when they in turn formed the Partido Comunista
    Venezolano.   The P. D. N. and the P. C. V. were both
    outlawed before the 1941 elections.

ORINOCO RIVER.   It was explored by Ordaz, 1531-1532.
    Alexander von Humboldt explored its upper reaches,
    discovering the linkage with the Amazon River system.
    The source of the Orinoco was not established until
    the 1931, 1943, and 1951 expeditions.   It first flows
    northwest, then north, and finally eastward to the
    Atlantic.   The main channel at the mouth, the Río
    Grande, is almost eighteen miles wide.   The delta
    has a seafront on the Atlantic Ocean of 265 miles.
    1, 344 miles long, it is second only to the Amazon in
    South America, draining most of Venezuela and offer-
    ing 1, 200 miles of navigation for light-draft vessels.

OTERO, ALEJANDRO, 1921- .   Abstractionist painter with
    a cool, precise, geometrical style.

OTOMAC INDIANS.   Neighbors to the Achagua in the llanos,
    their culture bore no resemblance to any other South
    American tribe.   Their day began in sorrow and ended
    in a festival which lasted until midnight.   The signal
    feature of their culture was that men, not women, did
    all of the farmwork.

OVIEDO Y BAÑOS, JOSE DE.   A member of the retinue of
    his uncle, the Bishop of Caracas, he only completed
    the first volume of his Historia de la conquista y
    población de la Provincia de Venezuela.

-P-

P. C. U.   see   PARTIDO COMUNISTA UNITARIO

P. C. V.   see   PARTIDO COMUNISTA VENEZOLANO

P. D. N.   see   PARTIDO DEMOCRATICA NATIONAL

P. D. V.   see   PARTIDO DEMOCRATICO VENEZOLANO

P. R. I. N.   see   PARTIDO REVOLUCIONARIO DE INTEGRA-
CION NACIONAL

P. R. N.   see   PARTIDO REVOLUCIONARIO NACIONALISTA

PACHANO, JACINTO REGINO, 1835-1903.   A Liberal who
served in 1854 under his friend Falcón, he has figured
in politics since the Federation.   There is hardly a
portfolio in the government that he did not have.   He
wrote a biography of Falcón, as well as other historical works.

PADRON, BALTASAR.   One of the three-man Executive that
was elected on 28 March 1811 to rule the newly-inde-
pendent country.

PADRON, JULIAN, 1910- .   Novelist whose works are usu-
ally set in eastern Venezuela.

PAEZ, JOSE ANTONIO, 1790-1873.   When he encountered a
slave revolt in 1809 at Las Huerfanitas, he assisted
and took over their leadership, starting a guerrilla
group.   He fought 1810-1813 in this manner and in
1815 led the llaneros to recover the province.   Swear-
ing allegiance to Bolívar in 1817 he continued in the
Wars of Independence until 1823.   He was responsible
for dislodging the last Royalist forces from Venezuela
soil at Puerto Cabello in 1823.   He was opposed to
the leadership of Santander and revolted against Bolívar first in 1826 and then in 1829.   A constitutional
convention that was called in 1830 made him the Republic's first President in 1831.   The constitution of
1830 returned the absolute control of political and eco
nomic affairs to the hands of the criollo landowners
and to the merchants.   His first term, 1831-1835,
was relatively peaceful.   After Vargas proved to be

unsuccessful, Páez was called from retirement to
serve again, 1839-1843. He had supported Vargas
and had defeated the rebels of the July, 1835 revolt.
As leader of the Conservatives he led the revolt
against José Tadeo Monagas in 1847. He was captured and imprisoned, 1847-1850. He returned from
exile in 1858, and was Minister to the United States
in 1860. In 1861 he was recalled to become President
with dictatorial powers. When the Federalists won
the war, he resigned in 1863 and was exiled to the
United States. He died there on 7 May 1873. He has
been called "Founder of the Venezuelan Nation. "

PAITITI. King· of Manoa, the fabulous domain which the
Spaniards called El Dorado: the hidden lake city with
golden turrets.

PALACIO FAJARDO, MANUEL, 1784-1819. Representative
to the Congress of 1811, he was a signer of the Venezuelan Declaration of Independence and the Constitution. He accompanied Miranda in the 1812 campaign
and then emigrated to Nueva Granada. Accepting foreign posts for Bolívar, he later returned to Venezuela
in 1818 and attended the Congress of 15 February
1819. On 27 February Palacio Fajardo was made
Secretary of State with the portfolios of Treasury and
Foreign Relations. He died on 8 May 1819.

PARTIDO COMUNISTA UNITARIO. After its split with U. P.,
it was led by Juan Bautista Fuenmayor in 1946. The
group was called the Red Communist Party.

PARTIDO COMUNISTA VENEZOLANO. Formed underground
in 1931 as a section of the Third International, its
leaders were: Rodolfo Quintero, Juan Bautista Tama-
yo, and Francisco José Delgado. In 1936 it began
again in Venezuela among the oil workers, but it was
outlawed by Gómez. In 1936-1937 it re-emerged in
the Partido Democrático Nacional, leaving in 1937 to
form its own group again. Legalized by Medina, it
took the name Unión Popular in 1941, but was outlawed before the elections. In 1942 it was again active underground among the oil workers and students.
In 1942-1943 pro-communist groups were formed, ap-
pearing under the name Unión Popular Venezolano
since the constitution forbade the Communist Party.
The 1945 amendment to the constitution allowed the

party to appear under its own name. It was outlawed
again in May, 1950. Active in 1958, it supported the
candidacy of Larrazábal. In 1960 it was joined by
M. I. R., the Marxist youth movement. Together they
launched an anti-government rural and urban guerrilla
warfare under the name of Fuerzas Armadas de Liberación Nacional. In 1962 its right to operate openly
was suspended and in 1963 it was outlawed again.
After 1966 P. C. V. sponsored nonviolent activities, although the F. A. L. N. still carried out guerrilla action. Leaders of the party are: Jesús Farías,
Gustavo Machado Morales, Pompeyo Márquez, Pedro
Ortega Díaz, Héctor Rodríguez Bauza, and Guillermo
García Ponce.

PARTIDO DEMOCRATICA NACIONAL. Regrouping in 1937
in O. R. V. E., it was outlawed before the 1941 elections. It became Acción Democrática.

PARTIDO DEMOCRATICO VENEZOLANO. Organized in 1936
by Betancourt in exile, it won an overwhelming majority in local government elections in 1945.

PARTIDO REPUBLICANO PROGRESISTA. Started by the
communists, circa 1935.

PARTIDO REVOLUCIONARIO DE INTEGRACION NACIONAL.
This political party was formed in July, 1966 from
Raul Rámos Giménez's Partido Revolucionario Nacionalista, Vanguardia Popular Nacionalista, and from
the soft-liners of M. I. R.

PARTIDO REVOLUCIONARIO NACIONALISTA. Formerly
A. D. -OP, it was led by Raul Rámos Giménez. It
joined with V. P. N. and the soft-liners of M. I. R. to
form P. R. I. N. in 1966.

PARTIDO SOCIAL CRISTIANO. Founded in 1946, its leader
was always Rafael Caldera Rodriguez who was its unsuccessful candidate for President in 1958 and 1963.
COPEI, as it is called, controlled three ministries
while in coalition with A. D. The party has the repu-
tation for being the best-educated party. There are
a large number of lawyers among its members. Originally it was very conservative, but it has moved left-
ward and now advocates a progressive program that
is consistent with Christian democratic reformism.

Traditionally its strength lies in the Andean states.
Since 1958 its strength has improved among middleclass women.   Caldera was elected President in 1968.

PATRIOTIC JUNTA.   Formed by all political parties in order
to overthrow Pérez Jiménez, it called a general strike
on 21 January 1958.   Pérez Jiménez resigned the next
day.   See JUNTA PATRIOTICA.

PATRIOTIC SOCIETY FOR AGRICULTURE AND ECONOMY.
Created on 14 August 1810 by a decree of the junta
in order to encourage agriculture and industry, it in
fact became a political club about 10 December 1810
when Bolívar joined it, along with Miranda.   The Society supported the idea of independence and became
a center of political agitation, putting pressure on the
Congress to persuade it to declare complete independence for the country.   El Patriota Venezolano became
the organ of the society.   The society sent a deputa-
tion to the Congress on 4 July 1811 to present its
ideas of independence.

PAUL, FELIPE FERMIN.   When the National Congress met
on 2 March 1811, its first president was Paúl, a member of the Patriotic Society.

PEÑA, MIGUEL, 1781-1833.   He was the leader of the dep-
utation from the Patriotic Society to the National Congress on 4 July 1811.   A member of the Supreme
Court of Justice, 1821-1825, he caused Valencia in
1826 to join with Páez against Bogotá.   In 1829 he
forced the citizen assembly in Valencia to insist upon
a separation from Gran Colombia and on 13 January
1830 he was a member of the cabinet that was set up
by Páez.   He was eventually replaced by Soublette as
the brain behind Páez.

PEÑALVER, FERNANDO DE, 1765-1837.   As President of
the Congress in January, 1812, he signed the Act of
Independence.   He was a member of Bolívar's Provisional Council of State of 30 October 1817 and a member of the Congress of Angostura in 1819.   He was
also a member of the Congress of Cúcuta in 1821.

PEREZ, JUAN BAUTISTA.   Gómez resigned and suggested
that this Supreme Court Judge succeed him in 1929.
Congress elected Pérez who served until 1931, when

Congress demanded that Gómez return.

PEREZ BONALDE, JOSE ANTONIO, 1846-1892. Lyric poet
   whose romantic plots are set in distant lands and not
   in Venezuela. He has a stylistic mixture of realism
   and naturalism in his poetry, along with the descrip-
   tive, picturesque passages.

PEREZ DE TOLOSA, JUAN. The Spanish governor, 1546-
   1548, he distributed the Indians in encomiendas to the
   conquistadores in order to work the mines and to cul-
   tivate the lands of the valleys. In 1547 he captured
   Carvajal and executed him. Reorganizing the province
   he left Juan de Villegas in charge while he went to re-
   organize Cabo de la Vela, where he died. He also
   sent his brother Hernán as far as Cúcuta, from which
   voyage he returned in 1550. Pérez de Tolosa was
   responsible for the expeditions that sought sites for
   San Cristóbal, Barquisimeto, and Valencia.

PEREZ JIMENEZ, MARCOS. 1914- . One of the officers
   who staged a coup to overthrow Medina Angarita in
   1945. On 18 October 1945 he was arrested by Medina
   Angarita, but on 19 October Medina Angarita surrendered to him. As an officer from Táchira, he was a
   member of the junta of 24 November 1948 that overthrew the government of Gallegos. He became dictator when Delgado Chalbaud was assassinated in 1950.
   On 2 December 1952 he proclaimed a F.E.I. victory,
   sent Llovera Páez and Suárez Flamerich abroad, and
   became Provisional President. The Constitutional Assembly granted him full powers in March, 1953. A
   spy and police organization was established and his
   opposition were either jailed or exiled. The Universidad Central was closed; the press was censored.
   There was a plebiscite on 15 December 1957 to determine whether he should continue as President. The
   Patriotic Junta overthrew the government on 22 January 1958. He escaped the country, but the United
   States returned him to Venezuela in 1963. He was
   placed in prison and eventually sentenced after years
   of trial. Exiled again in 1969, he won a seat in the
   Congressional elections of 1969, but the courts annulled his victory. During his rule the name of the
   country was changed in 1952 from the United States
   of Venezuela to the Republic of Venezuela.

95   Petroleum

PETROLEUM. The first commercial enterprise for the ex-
ploitation of oil in Venezuela was in 1878 when the
Compañía Petrolia del Táchira drilled in the Rubio
district of the State of Táchira. The production was
15 barrels daily at the end of the century, but by 1912
it rose to 60 barrels daily. The company subsequently failed. Important concessions were made to the
oil companies in 1907. In February permission was
given to Andrés Jorge Vigas to exploit the Colón district in Zulia; to Antonio Aranguren to exploit the
Maracaibo and the Bolívar districts. In July permission was given to Francisco Jiménez Arráiz in Falcón
and Lara; and to Bernabé Planas in Falcón. A contract was made in 1909 with the Venezuela Development Company, Ltd., which was represented by John
Allen Tregelles that practically covered the whole
country north of the Orinoco. This company also
went bankrupt. In 1910 the Bermúdez Company gained
concessions in Paria Peninsula, in the Benítez district of Sucre and in the Pedernales and adjacent islands in the Delta Amacuro territory. The Caribbean
Petroleum Company gained concessions in 1912. Actually Caribbean Petroleum was just a subsidiary of
the Royal Dutch Shell Group. Creole Petroleum Corporation, which began in 1920, eventually brought together all of the Standard operations. Venezuela is
the third largest oil-producing area in the world.
Most of the present Venezuelan oil is refined on the
islands of Aruba and Curaçao.

PIAR, MANUEL, 1780?-1817. In 1814 he and José Félix
Ribas threw Bolívar and Mariño into jail, Bolívar and
Mariño departing for Cartagena on 8 September 1814.
He disputed Bolívar's command again in 1815. In
1816-1817 he invaded Guayana, Bolívar joining him in
April, 1817. In 1817 Piar attempted to assume com-
mand of the patriots, working with Mariño, August-
September, 1817. Piar was captured and sent to An-
gostura where he was shot on 16 October 1817 as a
conspirator, rebel, and deserter.

PICON SALAS, MARIANO, 1901- . Three professorships,
two ambassadorships, and representation on the delegation to UNESCO. He has written many books,
among them: De la colonia a la independencia, Historia y proceso de la literatura Venezolana, and Comprensión de Venezuela.

PIMENTEL, ANTONIO. During the first quarter of the 20th century, this lascivious little man became, as a confidant to Gómez, the second richest man in Venezuela.

PLAZA, AMBROSIO, 1790-1821. He was killed at the battle of Carabobo on 24 June 1821 where he commanded one of the divisions of Bolívar's forces.

POCATERRA, JOSE RAFAEL, 1890- . He has written a number of novels and short stories about the people and life in different social strata of Valencia. Ironic, sarcastic and satirical, these works reflected the Russian realists. He was jailed toward the end of the Gómez regime and wrote only two books about his early prolific period. Memorias de un Venezolano en Decadencia (1927) related the corruption of the ruling class, its adulation of Gómez, and what the author believed was the inherent cruelty of the Venezuelan nature. He has been a member and President of the Senate, a minister, and several times has been an ambassador.

POLEO, HECTOR. One of the notable social painters, his best works date from the 1940's. He explores the expressive possibilities of strong color, patternistic composition, and simplified form. His canvasses have a surrealistic quality of fantasy.

PONTE, GABRIEL. One of the men generally thought responsible for the new constitution of 1811.

PRESIDENTS. The constitutional leaders [and presiding officials] of the Fourth Republic have been:
Jose Antonio Páez: 11 April 1831 - 20 January 1835.
Jose Vargas: 9 February 1835 - 24 March 1836. The Revolución de Reformas interrupted his regime.
Carlos Soublette: 24 April 1836 - January 1839.
Jose Antonio Páez: 1 February 1839 - 20 January 1843.
Carlos Soublette: 28 January 1843 - 20 January 1847.
Jose Tadeo Monagas: 1 March 1847 - 20 January 1851.
Jose Gregorio Monagas: 5 February 1851 - 20 January 1855.
Jose Tadeo Monagas: 31 January 1855 - 15 March

1858. The term ended with the triumph of the
Revolución de Marzo of Julián Castro.
Manuel Felipe de Tovar: 12 April 1860 - 20 May
1861.
[Pedro Gual: May, 1861 - August, 1861.]
[José Antonio Páez: August, 1861 - 1863.]
[Juan Crisóstomo Falcón: 1863 - 1865.]
Juan Crisóstomo Falcón: 7 June 1865 - 30 April
1868.
[José Tadeo Monagas: 28 June 1868 - November
1868.]
[José Ruperto Monagas: 8 March 1869 - 27 April
1870.]
[Antonio Guzmán Blanco: 1870 - 1873.]
Antonio Guzmán Blanco: 27 April 1873 - 20 Feb-
ruary 1877.
Francisco Linares Alcántara: 2 March 1877 - 30
November 1878.
[José Gregorio Varela: 1878 - 1879.]
Antonio Guzmán Blanco: 17 March 1880 - 1882.
Antonio Guzmán Blanco: 17 March 1882 - 1884.
Joaquín Crespo: 27 April 1884 - 1886.
Antonio Guzmán Blanco: 15 September 1886 - 1888.
Juan Pablo Rojas Paúl: 5 July 1888 - 1890.
Raimundo Andueza Palacio: 19 March 1890 - 1892.
[Joaquín Crespo: 1892 - 1894.]
Joaquín Crespo: 1894 - 20 February 1898.
Ignacio Andrade: 28 February 1898 - 1899. The
Revolución Liberal Restauradora led by General
Castro terminated his term.
Cipriano Castro: 1902 - 1908.
[Juan Vicente Gómez: 1908 - 1910.]
Juan Vicente Gómez: 27 April 1910 - 1914.
Juan Vicente Gómez: Elected 3 May 1913 for 1915 -
1922. Dr. Victorino Márquez Bustillos was Pro-
visional President during this period.
Juan Vicente Gómez: Elected May 1922 for 1922 -
1929.
Juan Bautista Pérez: 29 May 1929 - June 1931.
Juan Vicente Gómez: 13 July 1931 - 17 December
1935.
Eleazar López Contreras: 1 January 1936 for the
completion of Gómez's term.
Eleazar López Contreras: Elected May 1936 for the
period 1936 - 1941.
Isaías Medina Angarita: 5 May 1941 - 18 October
1945. Deposed by revolution.

Junta Revolucionaria, presided over by Rómulo Be-
tancourt: 1945 - 1948.
Rómulo Gallegos: 15 February 1948 - 24 November
1948.
Junta Militar, presided over by Carlos Delgado
Chalbaud: 24 November 1948 - 13 November
1950.
Junta, presided by Germán Suárez Flamerich: 27
November 1950 - 2 December 1952.
Marcos Pérez Jiménez: March 1953 - 1957.
Marcos Pérez Jiménez: December 1957 - 22 Jan-
uary 1958.
Junta Patriota, presided by Wolfgang Larrazábal: 22
January 1958 - 1959.
Junta, presided over by Edgar Sanabria: 1959.
Rómulo Betancourt: 13 February 1959 - 1964.
Raúl Leoni: 11 March 1964 - 1969.
Rafael Caldera: 11 March 1969 - [1974.]

PRESTON, AMYAS. He landed at La Guaira in 1595 and
marched on Caracas which he plundered for ten days.

PRIETO FIGUEROA, LUIS BELTRAN, 1902- . A member
of the executive committee of Orve, 1936, and of
Partido Democrático Nacional, 1937-1941, he was a
political prisoner, 1938-1941. He was second vice-
president of A.D., 1941-1945, and was the secretary
general of the Junta Revolucionaria which took over
the government in October, 1945. He was the President of the Senate 1963-1964 and in 1968 was the candidate for President of the People's Electoral Movement which had split from A.D.

LA PUERTA, BATTLES OF. On 2 February 1814 Boves
slaughtered the Patriot army which was commanded
by Vicente Campos Elías. On 15 June 1814 Boves
defeated Bolívar and Mariño. In December, 1901 the
government forces under Gómez crushed the rebels
during La Libertadora.

PULGAR, VENANCIO. General. He took Castle Libertador
and placed the garrison in the service of the Liberal
Revolution of 1870. He was a Senator for Falcón in
the Congress of 1890.

PULIDO, JOSE IGNACIO. Along with Generals Crespo, Salazar, and Colina, he rose in revolt on 27 April 1870

and called Guzmán Blanco back to lead. The Forces
of Regeneration took over the government and was the
last successful revolution for 20 years. He was an
unsuccessful candidate for President in 1872. In
1874-1875 he fought against Guzmán Blanco and was
sent into exile. In 1898 he was sent to Coro, in
Falcón, as the new chief of the second military region. When he clashed politically with General Gregorio Segura Riera, who was president of Falcón, he
was removed. Pulido supported Castro in 1899.

PULIDO, LUCIO. Liberal Deputy for the federal district in
the Congress of 1890. He was a member of the group
who proclaimed the federal revolution at Barinas.

-Q-

QUINTERO, ANGEL, 1805-1866. Deputy to the Congress of
Valencia in 1830, he was a staunch follower of Páez.
After being secretary to Páez, he became Minister of
Interior and Justice, 1839-1843, during which time he
was attacked by Guzmán in El Venezolano. He was
again named Minister in 1847, but he shortly renounced his portfolio. In 1849 he was part of the
Páez revolt against Monagas and was expelled for his
activities. He returned to Venezuela in 1861.

QUINTERO, JOSE HUMBERTO. Archbishop of Caracas, and
Cardinal.

QUIRIQUIRE INDIANS. Inhabiting the area east of Lake
Maracaibo, they were superior boatmen, engaging the
Spanish ships with clubs and arrows. During the
first years of the conquest they were wiped out by
the thousands, the rest being enslaved. They were
treated as cannibals and had a "C" burned into their
flesh by the Spaniards. They were lake dwellers who
built houses on piles for protection. In 1578 Garci-
González fought them.

-R-

RALEIGH, SIR WALTER. He seized and burned Cumaná.
In 1617 he sent an expedition up the Orinoco, seeking
El Dorado. His son was killed at San Tomé in a bat-

tle with Spanish ships.

RAMOS, JOSE LUIS, 1790?-1849. A self-taught classical
    scholar, he was the author of Spanish and Greco-
    Spanish grammars and dictionaries. He was one of
    the secretaries of the Congress of 2 March 1811. In
    1830 he became the director of public education.

RAMOS JIMENEZ (GIMENEZ), RAUL. When A.D. split in
    1961, he led the faction called A.D.-Ars which was a
    non-marxist leftist group.

RANGEL, FRANCISCO. In 1846 he rebelled against local
    election abuses and occupied Güigüe. He was known
    as El Indio.

REFORMS, WAR OF see WAR OF THE REFORMS

REGENERACION. Generals Pulido, Crespo, Salazar, and
    Colina rose in revolt and called Guzmán Blanco from
    Curaçao to lead them. On 27 April 1870 the Forces
    of Regeneration, as they called themselves, took Ca-
    racas.

REPUBLIC, FIRST see AMERICAN CONFEDERATION OF
    VENEZUELA

REPUBLIC, SECOND. On 8 August 1813 Bolívar re-entered
    Caracas. On 2 January 1814 the supreme power was
    given to Bolívar by the popular assembly. The gov-
    ernment was architected by Ustáriz. The Republic
    fell militarily by the end of 1814.

REPUBLIC, THIRD. On 7 May 1816 Bolívar was recognized
    at Villa del Norte as the Supreme Chief of the Repub-
    lic of Venezuela. In 1819 Bolívar resigned his dicta-
    torial power at the Congress of Angostura and was
    there named Provisional President of the Republic of
    Venezuela. Francisco Antonio Zea was named Vice-
    President, being given the executive power while Bo-
    lívar was in the field. In December, 1819, Bolívar
    founded the Republic of Colombia. Bolívar was elected
    President and Zea, Vice-President. Santander led the
    government of Cundinamarca and Juan Germán Roscio
    the government of Venezuela. After the battle of Ca-
    rabobo, which insured the separation of Venezuela's
    ties to Spain, Bolívar continued as the Supreme Pow-

er--the head of the government of Colombia (which
included the area of Venezuela)--and Carlos Soublette
assumed the Vice-Presidency for the Department of
Venezuela. At the end of the same year, Bolívar was
elected President of the newly formed country of Colombia at the Congress of Cúcuta. In 1822 Páez became Civil and Military Chief of the Department of
Venezuela. In 1830 Páez established a separatist government in Venezuela, removing the Department of
Venezuela from the confederation which was called the
Republic of Colombia, thereby dissolving the Republic
of Colombia.

REPUBLIC, FOURTH. Began 13 January 1830 when Páez
set up the provisional government, dissolving the Republic of Colombia.

RESTAURACION. Cipriano Castro entered Caracas on 22
October 1899 with the troops of the Restauración as
he called his crusade.

REVENGA, JOSE RAFAEL, 1781-1852. In 1810 he was
secretary to the mission that was sent to the United
States. He was also an emissary to London in 1822.
He was many times minister for Bolívar. In 1827 he
was Secretary General to Bolívar. Monagas in 1849
also selected him as minister.

REVERON, ARMANDO. In 1920 he left Caracas to spend
his remaining 34 years painting by the sea in a small,
primitive hut. He sought thereby to capture the brilliant white light of the tropics on canvas. His paint-
ings were dominated by light effects on figures,
forms, and landscapes.

RIBAS, JOSE FELIX, 1775-1815. Uncle of Bolívar and revolutionary patriot, he fought along side of Bolívar and
went to Nueva Granada in 1813. On 12 February 1814
he defeated Morales with a force of school-boys and
students. At the end of the Second Republic he, with
others, accused Bolívar of being a traitor. In September, 1814 he and Piar threw Bolívar in jail. In
the guerrilla resistance that followed the demise of
the Second Republic, Ribas was captured by Morales
and executed on 31 January 1815.

RIO Y CASTRO, ALONSO DEL. He was the Governor of

Margarita who was sent to Cumaná in 1759 to assume
the power of the residencia judge from Governor
Mateo Gual. He sentenced Gual to a minute fine for
not establishing prisons.

RODRIGUEZ, SIMON; or SIMON CARREÑO; or ROBINSON;
1771-1854. A follower of Rousseau, he was instrumental in shaping Bolívar's thinking. The 1797 España
revolt caused Rodríquez to leave Venezuela abruptly
since he was suspected of complicity. He was reunited with Bolívar in Europe in 1804. Twenty years
later he returned to South America, spending his last
years in areas other than Venezuela.

RODRIGUEZ, VICTOR. On 31 October 1899 Andrade fled
Caracas, leaving the Presidency to General Rodríguez
who was President of the Council of Government.
Rodríguez surrendered Caracas to Castro on the next
day.

RODRIGUEZ SUAREZ, JUAN. In 1558 he founded Mérida
during an expedition from Pamplona. He then went
further north into Trujillo where he met some coloni-
zers from El Tocuyo.

RODRIQUEZ, FRANCISCO see MARQUES DEL TORO

ROJAS, ARISTIDES, 1826-1894. He mingled history and
poetry in his Leyendas históricas de Venezuela and
his Estudios históricos. Orígenes Venezolanos.

ROJAS, CRISTOBAL, 1858-1890. Neoclassist painter, he
was a follower of Tovar y Tovar.

ROJAS, MIGUEL ANTONIO. As President of the State of
Aragua in December, 1867 he pronounced that he and
his friends had adopted a blue flag and were calling
themselves 'Reconquerers.' Aragua, Carabobo, and
Guárico rose in revolt. In February, 1868 José Tadeo
Monagas was placed in charge of the revolution. In
March, 1868 Rojas became commander-in-chief of the
original states where the revolution had started.

ROJAS, PEDRO JOSE. Faction under him in the Centralist
government brought Páez back to Venezuela in 1861
and installed Páez as dictator on 10 September 1861.
Rojas became Páez's only minister, devoting himself

to the treasury. He met with Guzmán Blanco in 1863
at the hacienda called Coche where the treaty was
drawn to end the hostilities.

ROJAS, PEDRO MANUEL. Liberal military leader in the
    east. Raimundo Andueza Palacio was his subsecre-
    tary.

ROJAS PAUL, JUAN PABLO. Liberal President, 5 July
    1888-1890, he was noted for progressive attitudes.
    He reinstated the freedom of the press. On 27 April
    1899, during the demonstrations by the opponents of
    Guzmán Blanco, he defended the statutes of Guzmán
    Blanco. Although Crespo staged an unsuccessful rev-
    olution against Rojas Paúl after the election of 1888,
    Crespo was won over by Rojas Paúl's openness and
    generosity. The Presidency was turned over peace-
    fully to his successor Raimundo Andueza Palacio.
    Rojas Paúl then became Senator for Bolívar, Cara-
    bobo, and Zamora and a Deputy for Falcón in the
    Congress of 1890.

ROMERO GARCIA, MANUEL VICENTE, 1865-1917. His
    Peonía (1890) is considered to be the first national
    novel of Venezuela. In it is the complete expression
    of an embryonic national tendency.

ROOKE, JAMES. Colonel of the British Legion in 1819.

ROSCIO, JUAN GERMAN, 1769-1821. In 1810 he was Secre-
    tary of State for Foreign Affairs for the Junta Supre-
    ma. He wrote the preamble and the regulations for
    the elections of the towns that were called for on 11
    June 1810. The Act of Independence was written by
    him and Iznardi. He served as a substitute in the
    provisional government of March, 1812. In 1817 he
    wrote El Triunfo de la libertad sobre el despotismo.
    A member of the Congress of 1819, he was appointed
    Vice-President of the Department of Venezuela in the
    provisional government, but he died before the govern-
    ment settled in Cúcuta in 1821. His treatises were
    written with the aim of providing juridical and philo-
    sophical bases for the new state.

-S-

SALAS, TITO, 1888- . Neoclassical painter who is a follower of Tovar y Tovar.

SALAZAR, MATIAS, 1828-1872. After the Federalists won
in the 1860's, he went to Cojedes where he played the
role of agitator, demagogue, leading politician, and
influential figure in the regional militia. In 1869 he
organized a guerrilla force to help Antonio Guzmán
Blanco. When Guzmán Blanco became Provisional
President, Salazar emerged as number three man.
He was foiled in an attempt to kill the President and
went to the United States. It is said that Don Felipé
Larrazábal, musician and author, persuaded Salazar
to rebel against Guzmán Blanco in 1872. Salazar was
captured in May, 1872 and was tried by a military
court of 23 generals-in-chief. He was convicted and
was executed on 17 May 1872.

SALIVA INDIANS. These Indians killed the first born of
twins because they believed that the husband could only
have sired one and that therefore the other was the
child of another man.

SALOM, BARTOLOME, 1780-1863. He fought in the Wars
of Independence from 1810 through the battle of Carabobo in 1821. Afterwards he went with Bolívar south
to Perú. Returning to Venezuela, he was an unsuccessful candidate for President in 1834 and supported
the constitution in the revolt of 1835. In the election
of 1846 Salom, as a Liberal candidate, had the majority of votes, but not the necessary two-thirds, so
Congress, under the influence of Páez, selected Monagas as President.

SALUZZO, MARCO ANTONIO, 1834-1912. A writer, poet,
and orator, he was Deputy for Barcelona in the constituent Congress of 1863 and a member of Congress
in 1865, 1866, and 1890. He was a charter member
of the National Academy of History.

SANABRIA, EDGAR. Head of the junta which took over from
the Larrazábal government, he in turn in 1959 handed
the government to Betancourt after the latter was
elected.

SANABRIA, MARTIN J., 1831-1904. In the government of
    Guzmán Blanco he held two ministries. He was a
    charger member of the National Academy of History
    in 1888 and was a Rector of the Central University.

SAN FELIPE. In 1741 the citizens of this city mutinied be-
    cause the Compañía Guipuzcoana tried to install one
    of its men as the city's chief judge. In the earth-
    quake of 26 March 1812 San Felipe vanished.

SAN FRANCISCO. Guaicaipuro, chief of the Teques, so ter-
    rorized this settlement that it was abandoned soon aft-
    er its founding in 1562. In 1567 Diego de Losada
    built a fort near the site of San Francisco and called
    the fort Santiago de León de Caracas.

SANTA INES, BATTLE OF. One of the two battles of the
    War of Federation. On 10 December 1859 Zamora
    beat the constitutional army which was commanded by
    Pedro Ramos.

SANTANDER, FRANCISCO DE PAULA, 1792-1840. He was
    named Vice-President of Cundinamarca by the Con-
    gress of Angostura. After the dissolution of Gran Co-
    lombia in 1830, he became President of Colombia,
    1831-1837.

SANTO TOME DE GUAYANA. Founded in 1590 by Berrío,
    it was originally the capital of Guayana. In 1768
    Angostura became the capital.

SANZ, MIGUEL JOSE, 1754-1814. One-time tutor to Bolívar
    and member of the aristocracy, he was a member of
    the Patriotic Society and also Secretary to the Con-
    gress of 1811. He was a political theorist of sound
    ideas and moral integrity. Unfortunately only three
    of his writings are known: his speech on the installa-
    tion of the Royal Academy of Public and Spanish Law
    in 1790; the essay on public education; and the bases
    for provisional government in 1813.

SARRIA, JULIO F. A Liberal who held many posts in the
    national militia, including Minister of War, he was a
    Deputy for Los Andes in the Congress of 1890.

SEDEÑO, ANTONIO. In 1530 he was Governor of Trinidad
    and also a royal treasury official in San Juan. He

later rebelled against the legitimate governor, Ortal, and against Juan de Frías who was sent by Santo Domingo to settle the quarrel. Sedeño died while he was seeking the Orinoco and Meta rivers.

SEGOVIA HIGHLANDS. Encompassing much of the States of Lara and Falcón, it is poor land: wild, deeply dissected plateaus from 6,000 feet in the south to 600 feet in the north.

SEGURA RIERA, GREGORIO. As President of the State of Falcón, he established himself as the leader of the party that his father had led. In 1898 he caused the removal of General Pulido when they clashed for political power in Falcón.

SEIJAS, RAFAEL, 1822-1901. Minister of Foreign Affairs in 1861, 1863, 1865-1866, 1868, 1878, 1880-1882, and 1890.

SEISSENHOFER, HANS. Called Juan Alemán, he became Governor of Coro after Alfinger. He scarely set foot outside of Coro during his short term.

SEMBRAR EL PETROLEO. This slogan, "sow the petroleum," was devised in the late 1930's to signify the practice of using petroleum profits to benefit social and economic projects.

SEMEN, BATTLE OF. On 16 March 1818 Bolívar was defeated by Morillo and Calzad.

SILVA, JOSE LAURENCIO, 1792-1873. Fighting in the Wars of Independence, he was expelled to the Antilles when Venezuela separated from Colombia. He was a reformist in 1835 and opposed Páez in 1849. In 1855 he became Minister of War and Navy.

SLAVES. Slavery was practiced by the Arawaks and Caribs. In the 16th Century the Indians were enslaved by the thousands by the Spaniards. The first Negroes were imported as slaves in 1528 when the first asiento was granted to the House of Welser, giving them the right to import 4,000 Negroes. These slaves came particularly from the Yoruba, Ibo, and Fon tribes. Bartolomé de las Casas had suggested the importation of Negroes under Crown control so that the Negroes

could be distributed to colonists who were willing to
accept the obligation of converting them to Christianity.   There was another shipment of Negro slaves in
1536.   During the 18th Century the Compañía Guipuzcoana brought in many shipments of slaves who became the labor force on the plantations, in the mines,
and in the homes.   One of the largest slave insurrec-
tions was led by a mixed breed, José Leonardo Chirino, at Coro in 1795.   The slave trade was officially
abolished by the Constitution of 1811, but was only
formally abolished in 1817.   The emancipation of the
slaves was suggested by Bolívar in 1819.   In 1821
children of slaves were born free, although they had
to work for their parents' masters until they became
18 years old.   On 24 March 1854 José Gregorio Monagas decreed the emancipation of the slaves.

SMALLPOX.   This disease was brought into Venezuela in
1580 by a Portuguese ship at Caraballeda.   By the
time the epidemic was spent, the majority of the Indians had disappeared.   Within a year the epidemic
had exterminated several large tribes in the Central
Valley.

SMITH, WILLIAM.   Surveyor of the Port of New York, he
recruited men for Miranda to invade Venezuela.   On
2 February 1806 the Leander sailed.   Smith and
Samuel Ogden were indicted for helping Miranda, but
they were eventually acquitted.   The invasion failed.

SOJO, PADRE PEDRO, 1739-1799.   Promoter of the musical
movement called "School of Chacao, " he traveled to
Europe for instruments and compositions.

SOJO, VICENTE EMILIO.   He helped found the choral group,
Orfeón Lamas, which stimulated the public interest in
music by bringing back old colonial compositions.   He
also helped promote the establishment of the Symphony
Orchestra, becoming its director.   He was director
of the National School of Music, founded in 1936.

SOREL, CAPTAIN JACQUES.   French freebooter who demanded 1000 pesos from the citizens of Borburata in
1567, threatening to burn the city if they refused.

SOSA RODRIGUES, CARLOS.   He was elected President of
the General Assembly of the United Nations for the

Eighteenth Session, 1963-1964.

SOTILLO, JUAN ANTONIO. Federalist leader on Trinidad
with Monagas in 1859, he invaded eastern Venezuela.
In February, 1860 Falcón joined with Sotillo and was
overtaken on 17 February 1860 by the Constitutional
forces which were commanded by Febres Cordero.
Falcón was completely defeated at Coplé.

SOTO, FRANCISCO DE. In 1520 Bartolomé de Las Casas
left de Soto to guard his interests near Cumaná. After Las Casas departed, de Soto subjected the Indians
to cruelty, using his ships to hunt slaves.

SOUBLETTE, CARLOS, 1789-1870. He joined the patriotic
movement in 1810 and served as aide-de-camp to
Miranda. Distinguishing himself in the battles of 1813,
and the siege of Cartagena in 1814, he became a
staunch supporter of Bolívar during the campaigns of
1816-1822. Bolívar left him as Vice-President of
Venezuela in 1821, and he thus became the constitutional chief of Venezuela after the war. When Páez
revolted in 1826, Soublette served Bolívar in Gran
Colombia. Nevertheless he supported Páez in 1829
and was a member of Páez's cabinet of 13 January
1830. In 1835 he was sent to Spain to conclude a
treaty of peace and commerce. Congress called upon
him to act as president when Vargas renounced his
office on 24 April 1836. Soublette held this interim
Presidency until January, 1839. He became President, 1843-1847. During his term there were economic crises, and the Venezuelan-Spanish peace treaty
was signed in 1845. Soublette was forced into exile,
1848-1858. When he returned under Julián Castro,
he defeated Falcón at La Guaira in 1858. He served
briefly as a minister under Gual in 1861.

SPIRA, JORGE; or GEORGE HOHERMUTH OF SPIERS. An
explorer of Venezuela after the period of Juan Alemán,
he left Coro in 1534 for El Dorado. He spent many
years exploring the Orinoco and Río Negro. He died
in 1540. His Lieutenant Governor was Nicolás Federmann.

STUDENT STRIKE OF 1928. The student body of the Central University in Caracas celebrated 6-12 February
1928 as student week. On Monday, 6 February the

students marched with a floral offering to the National
Pantheon where Jóvito Villalba attacked the govern-
ment in a speech.   The government quickly jailed
Vallalba and two other students.   The Federación de
Estudiantes sent delegations to the federal governor
to release the three students.   On 22 February the
Federación de Estudiantes sent an open telegram to
Gómez, challenging him to jail them also.   They announced that students agreeing with the declaration
would wear blue caps and F. E. V. buttons.   That night
more than 200 students were jailed in Puerto Cabello.
The jailing of the students caused reactions which co-
incided with or were the cause of the unsuccessful
army officer revolt of 7 April 1928.

SUAREZ FLAMERICH, GERMAN.   He was appointed as Provisional President in 1950 when Delgado Chalbaud was
assassinated.   In 1952 he was sent abroad by Pérez
Jiménez.

SUCRE, ANTONIO JOSE DE, 1795-1830.   A member of one
of the best families in eastern Venezuela, he joined
the independence movement in 1810, fighting under
Miranda in 1812 and contributing to Mariño's liberation of the east in 1813.   His devotion to duty and his
loyalty, personal charm, modesty, and courage made
him Bolívar's most trusted officer and friend.   He
initiated the conquest of Ecuador in November, 1820
and then went to Perú.   President of the Congress of
1830 in Bogotá, he was assassinated on 4 June 1830.

SUFFRAGE.   Limited suffrage was provided by decree on 13
January 1830 by Páez.   The election law of 1847 established universal suffrage.   Suffrage was granted to
women by Medina Angarita.

SUPREME JUNTA FOR THE CONSERVATION OF THE
RIGHTS OF FERDINAND VIII   see   JUNTA SUPREMA

-T-

TACHIRA.   Most important of the Andean valleys, it is
formed where the spine of the Andes crosses the gap
as a low saddle, thus dividing the rivers that flow
northward to Lake Maracaibo from the headwaters of
the Apure that flows eastward, becoming thereby one

of the main tributaries of the Orinoco. The fertile
valley of Táchira is almost agriculturally self-suffi-
cient. Traditionally Táchira is the seat of strong
regionalism, and for 46 years, 1899 to the end of
World War II, Tachirense caudillos controlled the national political scene.

TAGUANES, BATTLE OF. In July, 1813, 1, 200 Spaniards
left San Carlos for Valencia when Bolívar approached,
hoping by this move to join other Royalists for a last-
ditch stand. Bolívar selected 200 horsemen to head
the Royalists off. Riding through the night the calvary rode ahead of the Spaniards and blocked their path.
The next morning, 31 July, the calvary charged, sav-
agely battling the larger force which was commanded
by Colonel Izquierdo. Bolívar and the main force
then overtook and annihilated the 1, 200 Spaniards.

TELLERIAS. A family which used the resources of the State
of Falcón through the occupancy by them of the higher
and of many of the middle and lower posts of government of that state.

TENIENTE DEL REY. This position as the second ranking
official of the Province of Caracas was created in
Venezuela in 1778.

TEQUES INDIANS see GUAICAIPURO.

TIMOTE. The best known of the Andean chiefdoms, these
Indians were Arawak-speaking. They had the most
advanced culture of the Venezuelan Indians. Living
in the areas near present-day Mérida, they constructed their villages with a temple in the center and
their stone-walled houses grouped in orderly rows
around the temple. They worshipped a supreme being
who lived in the mountains and in the lakes. They
were intensive farmers whose irrigation system rep-
resents a unique achievement in Venezuelan Indian
culture. They did not practice human sacrifice.

TOCUYITO, BATTLE OF. In 1899 Castro made a stand
south of Valencia and pulverized his enemy. Valencia,
the second city in Venezuela, then became his. To
all intents and purposes the campaign was then over
as Andrade began to lose control of his supporters.

111 El Tocuyo

EL TOCUYO. Generally, El Tocuyo was a Spanish stronghold. It was founded by Carvajal who was later hanged from the gallows here by Governor Juan Pérez de Tolosa. In February, 1547 Alonso Pérez departed from here to discover the Santiago valley. Diego de Losada in 1567 marched from here eastward towards the site of San Francisco where he built a fort, calling it Santiago de León de Caracas.

TORO, FERMIN, 1807-1865. Greatest intellectual figure of his generation, he did not return to his seat in Congress after the assault of 24 January 1848. As a Conservative, he helped oust Monagas in 1858 and became a member of Castro's cabinet. He dispersed ideas on the ills of Venezuela, on English utilitarianism, and on jurisprudence in articles, speeches, and in essays. His fiction and poetry reflect his fascination for the romantics and his feeling for history. Among his works are: La Sibila de los Andes; La Viuda de Corinto; and Reflexiones sobre La ley del 10 de abril de 1834.

TORO, MARQUES DEL. Simón Bolívar married the Marqués' niece in 1802. The Junta Suprema appointed him as chief of the army of the west. In November, 1810 he reached Coro with his army, but was defeated, Coro remaining Royalist. He was defeated again at Valencia and was replaced then by Miranda. With Miranda he marched on Valencia in July, 1811. He later became known as Francisco Rodríquez and became a founder of the Liberal Party.

TORO Y ALAYSA, MARIA TERESA DE. A niece of the Marqués del Toro, she was 20 months older than Simón Bolívar whom she married. In June, 1802 Bolívar and his bride sailed from Europe for Venezuela, but within six months she was dead of yellow fever.

TORRE, MIGUEL DE LA, d.1838. A lieutenant of Morillo, he campaigned in Guayana in 1817. When Morillo departed, de la Torre became the Royalist leader in Venezuela. In 1821 he commanded the Royalist troops, with Morales as his second-in-command. He was defeated by Bolívar at Carabobo on 24 June 1821 and retreated to Puerto Cabello until its surrender on 10 November 1821. Afterwards he was appointed as civil and military governor of Puerto Rico in 1823 and

proclaimed the Spanish Constitution of 1837 on that
island. He received the title of Count of Torrepando.

TORRES, PEDRO LEON, 1788-1822. Fighting for the patriots in 1811, he was imprisoned in Puerto Rico in
1812. After the campaigns of 1813-1814 and the second battle of La Puerta he emigrated with Urdaneta
to Nueva Granada. In 1816-1817 he was with Piar
and made the llanos campaign with Bolívar in 1818.
He was killed on 7 April 1822 at the battle of Bombo-
ná.

TORRIJOS, BISHOP MANUEL CANDIDO. In 1794 he established the first laboratory of experimental physics at
the Seminary of Mérida.

TOSTA GARCIA, FRANCISCO. He attracted displeasure, as
a Liberal, of the revived Monagas regime, 1868-1870,
and had to leave Caracas. He became secretary to
General Desiderio Escobar and within a few days became his second in command, aiding in the capture
of Caracas in 1870. His is known for his Don Se-
gundino en Paris and his Costombres Caraqueños.

EL TOTUMO. The name of the declaration of 20 February
1892 wherein Joaquín Crespo, questioning the acts of
President Andueza Palacio, started the revolution of
1892.

TOVAR, MANUEL FELIPE DE. One of the founders of the
Liberal Party, he later returned to the Conservative
Party proposing to oust Monagas. In August, 1859
Julián Castro was ousted and Tovar, who was Vice-
President, was declared the President by the Con-
servatives. Gual presided over the government until
Tovar returned to Caracas in September. In April,
1860 Tovar became the constitutional President. When
he refused to become a dictator, a faction under
Pedro José Rojas brought Páez back to Venezuela.
Tovar resigned in May, 1861 and Vice-President Gual
became President. On 29 August 1861, Gual was
thrown into jail and Páez became dictator.

TOVAR FAMILY. In 1858 they were still rated the largest
landowners in Venezuela despite the Wars of Independence and the subsequent civil conflicts.

113   Tovar y Tovar, Martín

TOVAR Y TOVAR, MARTIN, 1828-1902. Called at the end
    of his life "the master of Venezuelan painting, " he
    was the official artist of the Gómez regime. He was
    dependent upon official commissions for his livelihood.
    His battle scenes depicted, in classical allegory, the
    important figures of the past and of the present public
    life.

TREE. The national tree is the Araguaney (Tecoma Chysantha).

LAS TRINCHERAS, BATTLE OF. Bolívar defeated Monte-
    verde decisively on 3 October 1813 here. Monteverde
    was forced to retreat again to Puerto Cabello.

TUY RIVER. It drains Caracas and the eastern end of the
    intermontane basin. Cacao is the dominant crop of
    the valley along the river.

                              -U-

U. P. see UNION POPULAR

U. P. M. see UNION PATRIOTICA MILITAR

U. R. D. see UNION REPUBLICANA DEMOCRATICA

UNION NACIONAL REPUBLICANA. In the mid-1930's this
    was the party favored by professional men, bankers,
    and businessmen.

UNION PATRIOTICA MILITAR. Secret organization of mili-
    tary officers in 1945 who offered support to A. D.
    when the latter opposed Medina Angarita. They thus
    helped overthrow the Medina Angarita regime. In
    November, 1948 they sent Gallegos an ultimatum for
    a coalition government with COPEI, but he refused.
    The army then deposed him.

UNION POPULAR. The communists formed a party in 1931,
    but it was banned in 1937. Legalized by Medina
    Angarita, it emerged as Unión Popular in 1941. The
    U. P. was known as the Black Communists when it
    split with the P. C. U. The party was led by Gustavo
    Machado Morales.

UNION REPUBLICANA DEMOCRATICA. Founded on 12

March 1946 by Jóvita Villalba, Dionisio López Ori-
huela, Enrique Betancourt Galíndez, and Luis Mique-
lena, its program is to work for national integration
by means of a coalition among parties and independ-
ents. It won the national elections of 1952, but the
results were nullified by Pérez Jiménez. In 1958 its
candidate for President was the president of the provisional government, Wolfgang Larrazábal. After
leaving the coalition with A. D. and COPEI in 1960,
it moved into active opposition, aligning itself on many
issues with the communist party and M. I. R. During
the 1963 campaign Villalba, its Presidential candidate,
adopted an independent stance. U. R. D. joined the
coalition government with A. D. and F. N. D. In 1966
a faction led by Ugarte Pelayo split off. Villalba was
again the unsuccessful candidate for President in 1968.
Today the political ideology of U. R. D. is not much
different from that of A. D.

UNITARIAN COMMUNIST PARTY   see   PARTIDO COMUNISTA
UNITARIO

UNITED STATES OF VENEZUELA.   The name of the republic after the Constitution of 1864.

UNIVERSIDAD CATOLICA ANDRES BELLO.   Founded at
Caracas.

UNIVERSIDAD CENTRAL DE VENEZUELA.   Founded by
Royal decree in 1721 and granted by the Pope on 19
August 1922, it was installed on 11 August 1725 with
a curricula of theology, philosophy, canon law, civil
law, and cases of conscience. Its name was Real y
Pontífica Universidad de Santiago de León de Caracas. Guzmán Blanco reformed the university in 1870,
emphasizing the sciences and bringing in foreign pro-
fessors. The 1928 student strike was a cause cé-
lèbre.

UNIVERSIDAD DE CARABOBO.   Established in 1852 at Valencia.

UNIVERSIDAD DE LOS ANDES.   Founded in 1810 at Mérida.
It was established in 1785 as Real Colegio Seminario
de San Buenaventura de Mérida.

UNIVERSIDAD DE ORIENTE.   Established in 1958 at Cumaná.

115   Universidad de Santa María

UNIVERSIDAD DE SANTA MARIA.   Founded in 1953 at Cara-
    cas.

UNIVERSIDAD NACIONAL DE ZULIA.   It was founded in
    1891 at Maracaibo.   It was closed in 1904, but re-
    opened in 1946.

URBANEJA, DIEGO BAUTISTA.   When Bolívar was elected
    President in 1819, Urbaneja became Minister of Inte-
    rior and Justice.   He was a member of Páez's cabi-
    net of 13 January 1830 and was Vice-President,
    March, 1831-February, 1835.   Vice-President again
    during the Monagas term in 1847, he is reputed to
    have told President Monagas that the constitution may
    serve any purpose.   This statement gave rise to the
    phrase "Urbanejismo" which connotes the intellectual
    who adjusts the laws to the will of a strongman or
    who advises him to rebel or to alter the public order.

URBANEJA ACHELPOHL, LUIS.   He combined modernism
    and realism into a synthesis which set the course of
    prose narrative.   In En este país he opted in favor
    of a new, willful, dynamic society of change and pro-
    gress over the cultured aristocracy.   He elevated
    costumbrista pieces and criollo themes to true short
    stories.

URBINA, RAFAEL SIMON.   This general became a national
    hero when he battled Gómez in the 1920's and 1930's.
    In early 1929 he launched an invasion from Curaçao.
    In order to prevent interference from the Dutch he
    kidnapped the governor of the island.   He then forced
    an American ship to take his force to the State of
    Falcón.   As the tiny army marched on Coro, the gov-
    ernment forces destroyed it, although Urbina escaped.
    In 1950 he helped murder Carlos Delgado Chalbaud.

URDANETA, RAFAEL, 1788-1845.   He campaigned through-
    out the Wars of Independence, being chief of staff to
    Bolívar in 1813, emigrating to Nueva Granada, and
    returning to aid Venezuela.   In the 1820's he was in
    Gran Colombia and was a member of the Congress of
    1830.   Returning to Venezuela, he upheld the constitu-
    tion in the revolution of the reformists.   In 1837 he
    was a member of Congress as well as a minister.
    He was also a minister in 1843-1845.   He died in
    Paris in 1845 while attempting to secure a loan that

the Conservatives hoped to finance the emancipation of
the slaves.   The Conservatives had hoped to run his
candidacy for President that year.

URPIN, JUAN DE.   During the 1636-1640 conquest of the
Cumaná Indians, he founded the town of Barcelona.

URRUTIA, WENCESLAO.   As a Liberal leader in 1858, he
proposed to oust Monagas.   When José Tadeo Monagas
took refuge in the French Embassy, Urrutia, the Venezuelan Foreign Minister, guaranteed Monagas' safe
passage out of the country.   The act made the country
furious and he was forced to resign.

USLAR PIETRI, ARTURO, 1906- .   A historian and literary
figure, he has had three ministries, three professorships, was a national Senator, and has been secretary
to the President of the Republic.   He was a candidate
in 1963 for the Presidency, representing I. P. F. N.
The party's name was changed on 25 February 1964
to Frente Nacional Democrática.   After his coalition
with A. D. and U. R. D. he was severely criticized by
his early backers.   In his early novel, 1931, Las
Lanzas coloradas he dealt with the Wars of Independence in a vivid and lyrical manner, painting the
masses that composed the rebellious colony.

USTARIZ, FRANCISCO JAVIER.   A member of provisional
government of March, 1812, while the Constitution of
1811 was being approved, he was placed by Miranda
in charge of the defense of Valencia.   He evacuated
the capital when Monteverde advanced in 1812 and was
later defeated by Boves in the llanos.   In 1814 he
produced the plan for provisional government which
gave Bolívar dictatorial power until the country became freed of the enemies within its territory.

-V-

VALLIERS, NICHOLAS.   A French freebooter who burned
Borburata in 1567 and sacked Coro when the Governor
there refused to give him permission to trade.

VARELA, JOSE GREGORIO.   While Guzmán Blanco was minister to various European countries, Linares Alcántara, the interim President, died in office in 1878.

The anti-Guzmán Blanco forces chose the illegitimate
brother of Linares Alcántara, José Gregorio Varela,
to succeed him.   General Cedeño rebelled in 1879 and
urged Guzmán Blanco to return home.   Varela was
thus President, 1878-1879.

VARGAS, JOSE, 1786-1854.   A candidate of the anti-military
    civilians, he was a professor at the University of
    Caracas when he was elected President.   He took of-
    fice in February, 1835, resigning several times but
    Congress did not accept his resignations.   Mariño and
    the officers revolted in June, 1835 and kidnaped
    Vargas on 8 July 1835, shipping him to the Virgin
    Islands.   Páez marched to save the government and
    within two weeks defeated the revolutionaries every-
    where but in Puerto Cabello which eventually surren-
    dered in February, 1836.   Vargas was reinstated as
    President in August, 1835, but he resigned on 24
    March 1836 because of a misunderstanding with the
    Congress.   Vice-President Soublette succeeded him as
    President.

VARGAS, MARIO.   As a captain, he was a member of the
    Junta Revolucionaria in 1945.   He was idealistically
    in sympathy with A. D.   Dying from tuberculosis, he
    left a sanatorium in the United States in order to join
    Delgado Chalbaud in a late attempt to mediate the dif-
    ferences between A. D. and the army.   He finally
    sided with the military.

EL VENEZOLANO.   The Liberal Party in 1840 established
    this newspaper to express their views.   Its editor
    was Antonio Leocadio Guzmán who from its pages de-
    manded universal suffrage, immediate emancipation
    of the slaves, and abolition of capital punishment for
    political crimes.   Within a few months of the found-
    ing, the Liberal backers withdrew their support from
    the paper because of Guzmán's views.

VENEZUELAN INCIDENT, FIRST.   In 1814 Holland ceded
    the western part of its Guiana territory to Great Brit-
    ain.   By 1840 the British had surveyed and marked
    the western boundary with a northern terminus on the
    eastern mouth of the Orinoco.   Venezuelan protests
    resulted in a succession of alternative proposals, but
    in no agreement.   Britain refused to submit the mat-
    ter to arbitration.   After gold was discovered in the

disputed territory, Venezuela severed diplomatic relations in 1877 with Britain. In April, 1895 border
guards arrested two minor British officials on the
Cuyuni River, charging them with a violation of Venezuelan territory. A threat of warships caused their
release, but public opinion was aroused. President
Cleveland denounced Britain, saying that our duty under the Monroe Doctrine was to determine the boundary and to resist British aggression. Since Britain
was involved in competition with France and Germany
in Africa and in the Middle East, she agreed to arbitration. The 1899 decision established the boundary,
Venezuela receiving control of the eastern mouth of
the Orinoco. Since the Chief Justice of the United
States had presented their case, the Venezuelans did
not believe that rights were well protected, although
they agreed to the decision. The Guiana boundary
problem essentially established the principle under the
Monroe Doctrine that the United States would intervene
on the behalf of any American state that is threatened
from abroad.

VENEZUELAN INCIDENT, SECOND. In 1902, during the
regime of Cipriano Castro, Britain and Germany
joined in an ultimatum to Venezuela in order to collect claims of debts. Upon Castro's rejection of their
demands, British and German warships seized or sank
a few vessels of the Venezuelan navy and bombarded
Puerto Cabello. These ships were joined later by the
Italian warships and they blockaded the whole Carrib-
bean coast of Venezuela. Whereas the United States
was inclined at first to side with the creditors, other
Latin American republics expressed a protest in the
form of the Drago Doctrine which was sent to Washington in December, 1902. This document suggested
that no public debt should be collected by an armed
force from a sovereign American state or through the
occupation of American territory by a foreign power.
President Theodore Roosevelt intervened to break the
blockade and to send the question of the claims against
Venezuela to the World Court at The Hague which decided that the intervening powers should have first
priority in the claims against Venezuela. President
Roosevelt then adopted the Drago Doctrine in a state-
ment in 1904 and amplified it in 1905 to bar intervention in America by an European power, but reserving
that right to the United States. This was known as

the Roosevelt Corollary to the Monroe Doctrine. In
1904 the World Court awarded the claimants (England,
Germany, Italy, Holland, France, Spain, Belgium,
Norway, Sweden, Mexico, and the United States) approximately one-fifth of the original claims. The
United States had the responsibility of the collection.
Another consequence of the Second Venezuelan Incident
was known as the Calvo Clause which required foreign
companies to waive the right to involve their government's diplomatic intervention should disputes occur
over their contract. This principle was reaffirmed
in the Venezuelan Constitution of 1961.

VERA, DOMINGO DE. In 1595 he attempted unsuccessfully
to settle in Santo Tomé and its district.

VERGARA, JUAN DE. He formed a partnership with Alonso
de Ojeda and García de Ocampo in order to raise capital for the 1502 voyage. When the expedition arrived
at Lake Maracaibo, Vergara and Ocampo accused Ojeda of stealing and carried him in chains to Hispaniola
for trial. Ojeda was eventually cleared of the charges.

VESPUCCI, AMERICUS. His four (three?) letters describing
the New World became influential in the 16th Century.
He visited Venezuela and Lake Maracaibo with Alonso
de Ojeda in 1499.

LA VICTORIA, BATTLE OF. In October-November, 1901
the government forces defeated the forces of the Liberating Revolution.

"VIERNES" GROUP. Named for the magazine (begun in 1939)
which sought to dignify poetry and to introduce new
trends, this group desired to move as far and as
quickly as possible from past traditions. Two of the
active participants were Vicente Gervasi and Otto de
Sola. The magazine quickly disappeared and the group
disintegrated.

VILLALBA, JOVITO, 1908- . With two other students from
the University of Caracas he made liberal, anti-government speeches on 6 February 1928. The jailing of
these students caused mobs to demonstrate in the
streets. A few army officers joined the students and
attempted to revolt on 7 April 1928. A student strike
was called, but Gómez closed the university, rounded

up the students, and placed them on road gangs.
Some students died in prison, others were held for
years, and still others left the country. On 14 February 1936 Villalba, as the head of the Federación de
Estudiantes, led 30,000 Caraqueños on the Miraflores
Palace to protest the shooting by troops under orders
of Félix Galavís, Governor of the Federal District.
General López Contreras submitted to their demands.
Villalba became the secretary general of Partido Democrático Nacional in 1936 and later became a national Senator. He was leader of U.R.D. and was its
unsuccessful candidate for President in 1963 and 1968.

VILLALOBOS, MARCELO DE. A judge in Hispaniola since
1511, he was given Margarita for a new Governorship
in 1525, but he died before taking possession. In
1527 his daughter, Aldonza, became Governor, although she was represented by a guardian because she
was a minor.

VILLANUEVA, CARLOS RAUL. He is an architect who
created the College of Architecture at the Central University of Caracas in the 1940's. He founded and
was the first president of the Venezuelan Society of
Architects. He has also exerted influence through his
position as counselor to the Banco Obrero, the principal constructor of low-cost housing projects, and
through his position as director of the Commission of
Urbanization. The Central University has been rebuilt under his direction.

VILLANUEVA, LAUREANO, 1840-1912. A medical doctor
who introduced the dosimetric system in Venezuela,
he edited with Raimundo Andueza Palacio, El Pabellón
de abril and El Demócrata during the administration
of Linares Alcántara. He was a Deputy for Zamora
in the Congress of 1890 and later became Rector of
the Central University.

VILLEGAS, JUAN DE. When Pérez de Tolosa executed
Carvajal, he reorganized the province and left Villegas in charge while he went to Cabo de la Vela where
he died. Villegas governed well and was appointed
Governor in 1548. He governed according to Spanish
norms although still in the name of the Welsers. He
discovered the earliest gold mines at Borburata.

-W-

WAR OF FEDERATION   see   FEDERAL WAR

WAR OF INDEPENDENCE, 1810-1821   see   Names of indi-
    viduals involved.

WAR OF THE REFORMS.   In 1835 the election of Vargas
    was the occasion for a military revolt.   It was the
    plotting of the Bolivarians, of the inactive status of-
    ficers, that stimulated the junior officers of the
    Anzoátegui Battalion to an unsuccessful rebellion
    against Vargas.   This caused José Tadeo Monagas to
    lead the rebellion.   The Valencia garrison joined the
    Bolivarians.   The rebellion in Maracaibo had preceded
    that of Caracas.   Some attribute the rebellion to the
    maneuver of Páez to prove himself indispensable for
    public peace; others to a Caracan alliance of Bolivarian
    monarchists and democrats; and still others to mili-
    tary ambition.   Páez conciliated the Monagan sector
    of the rebellion and defeated the Bolivarian sector,
    thus confirming his personal authority over the second
    administration of Venezuela that opened under Dr.
    Vargas.   222 persons were sent into exile and the
    army was reduced.   A number of fortifications were
    demolished because it was too costly to maintain them.
    Vargas later resigned and Páez's collaborator, Sou-
    blette, became President in 1837.

WAR TO THE DEATH.   The most important document of the
    1813 campaign was Bolívar's decree which was signed
    by him as Commander-in-Chief of the Army of the
    North at Trujillo on 15 June 1813.   It stated that the
    army was sent by the Congress of Nueva Granada to
    liberate Venezuela, that the patriot government of the
    Confederation of 1811 would be destroyed, and that it
    was necessary to rid the country of all Peninsulars.
    The decree completely separated the Americans from
    the Spaniards, distinguishing who were the Royalists.
    The armistice on 26 November 1820 effectively put an
    end to the War to the Death.   The War to the Death
    had been in existence practically from the penal de-
    cree of 16 April 1812 which threatened all the ene-
    mies of Venezuela with death, and also from the 16
    January 1813 agreement, as signed by Briceño, that
    stipulated that all Spaniards whether guilty or not

would be shot.

WELSERS. German banking house to whom Charles I of
Spain leased Venezuela in 1528 with the right to found
cities, to open mines, and to take slaves. The lease
was revoked in 1546 and officially ended in 1556.

WORLD WAR I. Gómez kept Venezuela neutral during this
war.

WORLD WAR II. Venezuela declared war on the Axis powers in February, 1945. She thus qualified for charter
membership in the United Nations.

-Y-

YANES, FRANCISCO JAVIER, 1785-1842. A member of the
Patriotic Society in 1810, he fought in the various
campaigns during the Wars of Independence. In 1824
he wrote Manual político de Venezuela which covered
the doctrines of republican government, the principles
of political philosophy of federalism, and the concepts
of liberty, equality, and private property. He later
wrote with Cristóbal Mendoza, Los Documentos para
la vida pública de Bolívar.

YAÑEZ PINZON, VICENTE. He accompanied Columbus on
the first voyage and then in December, 1499 left
Spain for another voyage. He reached the coast of
Brazil, then turned northward, sailing up the eastern
coast of Venezuela, and returned to Spain in September, 1500. He had seen the mouths of the Orinoco.
He was awarded with the title of governor of the lands
that he had discovered, but he never took possession.

YARURO. Aquatic nomads who lived on fish, turtles, and
riparian mammals, these Indians lived on the tributaries of the Orinoco and were reluctant to travel on
land.

YELLOWS. The Opponents of the Monagas Liberal-Conserva-
tive front in 1868. At first the yellow color stood
for Liberals.

YEPES, JOSE RAMON, 1822-1881. National Senator and
Deputy and naval officer, he is the most popular of

the Zuliano poets.

-Z-

ZAMORA, EZEQUIEL. 1817-1860. Until 1846 he was a
    merchant, being a Liberal candidate in the 1846 elec-
    tions. After quarreling with the election judge, he
    sold his store and became a guerrilla. He was cap-
    tured in 1847, but escaped in 1848, joining Monagas.
    Returning to farming in the Coro area, he became an-
    noyed when Julián Castro seized the government in
    1858. Zamora and Falcón, his brother-in-law, organ-
    ized the Federal Movement and went into exile. They
    returned to initiate the Federal War, 1859-1864. Za-
    mora defeated the constitutional army at Santa Inés on
    10 December 1859. He was killed at the battle of
    San Carlos on 10 January 1860.

ZEA, FRANCISCO ANTONIO, 1770-1822. Appointed by Napo-
    leon, he was the director-general of the Ministry of
    the Interior in Bonapartist Spain, 1808-1812. In 1819
    he was Vice-President of the Angostura Congress, be-
    ing instrumental in the charter for Gran Colombia.
    In September, 1819 he was replaced as Vice-President
    by Arismendi, and he went with Bolívar to Nueva Gra-
    nada. Zea was then sent to London to attempt to gain
    recognition for Gran Colombia, to negotiate a loan,
    and to fund the public debt.

ZORCA INDIANS. Their culture approximated the advance-
    ment of the Timotes. This tribe betrothed their chil-
    dren at birth.

Bibliography

Academia Nacional de la Historia. Biblioteca de la Academia Nacional de la Historia [Series contains many important bibliographical volumes.]

Academia Nacional de la Historia. Fuentes para la historia colonial de Venezuela. [Series contains many important bibliographical volumes.]

Academia Nacional de la Historia. Mesa Redonda de la Comisión de Historia del Instituto Panamericano de Geografía e Historia. El movimiento emancipador de Hispanoamérica. Actas y ponencias. Caracas, 1961. 4 vols.

Acedo Mendoza, Carlos. Venezuela: ruta y destino. Barcelona, Ediciones Ariel, 1966.

Acosta Saignes, Miguel. Elementos indígenas y africanos en la formación de la cultura venezolana. Caracas, Universidad Central de Venezuela, 1955.

Acosta Saignes, Miguel. Estudios de etnología antigua de Venezuela. Caracas, Ediciones de la Biblioteca, Universidad Central de Venezuela, 1961.

Acotaciones bolivarianas. Decretos marginales del Libertador (1813-1830). Caracas, Fundación John Boulton, 1960.

Aguirre Elorriaga, Manuel. La Compañía de Jesús en Venezuela. Caracas, Editorial Condor, 1941.

Aldrey, Fausto Teodoro de and Rafael Hernández Gutiérrez. Rasgos biográficos para la historia de la vida pública del General Guzmán Blanco. Caracas, Imprenta de "La Opinión Nacional" por F. T. de Aldrey, 1876.

Alexander, Robert Jackson. The Venezuelan Democratic Revolution. New Brunswick, N. J., Rutgers University Press, 1964.

Alfonso, Luis Jerónimo. Breve análisis del pasado de Venezuela. Caracas, Imprenta Nacional, 1872.

Alonso, Isidoro et al. La iglesia en Venezuela y Ecuador.
Freiburg, Switzerland, Federación Internacional de
los Institutos Católicos de Investigaciones Sociales y
Socio-religiosos, 1961.

Alvarado, Lisandro. Historia de la revolución federal en
Venezuela. Caracas, Ministerio de Educación, Dirección de Cultura y Bellas Artes, Comisión Editora
de las Obras Completas de Lisandro Alvarado, 1956.

Andara, José Ladislao. De política e historia. Curaçao,
Imprenta del Comercio, 1904.

Andara, José Ladislao. La evolución social y política de
Venezuela. Caracas, 1899.

Arcaya, Pedro Manuel. Estudios de sociología venezolana.
Caracas, Editorial Cecilio Acosta, 1941.

Arcaya, Pedro Manuel. Estudios sobre personajes y hechos
de la historia venezolana. Caracas, Tipografía
"Cosmos," 1911.

Arcaya, Pedro Manuel. Historia del Estado Falcón, República de Venezuela. Caracas, Tipografía La Nación,
1953.

Arcaya, Pedro Manuel. Venezuela y su actual régimen.
Baltimore, Baltimore Sun Printing Office, 1935.

Arcila Farías, Eduardo. Economía colonial de Venezuela.
México, Fondo de Cultura Económica, 1946.

Arcila Farías, Eduardo. El real consulado de Caracas. Caracas, Instituto de Estudios Hispanoamericanos, 1957.

Arcila Farías, Eduardo. El régimen de la encomienda en
Venezuela. Sevilla, Escuela de Estudios Hispano-
Americanos, Consejo Superior de Investigaciones
Científicos, 1957.

Arellano Moreno, Antonio. Documentos para la historia

económica de Venezuela. Caracas, Instituto de Antropología e Historia, Facultad de Humanidades y Educación, Universidad Central de Venezuela, 1961.

Arellano Moreno, Antonio. Fuentes para la historia económica de Venezuela, siglo XVI. Caracas, Tipografía "El Compás, " 1950.

Arellano Moreno, Antonio. Guía de historia de Venezuela, 1492-1945. Caracas, Ediciones Edime, 1955.

Arellano Moreno, Antonio. Orígenes de la economía venezolana. 2d ed. Caracas, Ediciones Edime, 1960.

Arévalo Cedeño, E. El libro de mis luchas. Caracas, Tipografía Americana, 1936.

Armas Chitty, José Antonio de. Tucupido: formación de un pueblo del llano. Caracas, Universidad Central de Venezuela, 1961.

Arráiz, Antonio. Geografía económica de Venezuela. Caracas, Cultural Venezolana, 1956.

Baralt, Rafael María. Resumen de la historia de Venezuela desde el año de 1797 hasta el de 1830. Brujas, Paris, Desclée, de Brouwer, 1939. 2 vols.

Baralt, Rafael María. Resumen de la historia de Venezuela desde el descubrimiento de su territorio por las castellanos en el siglo XV, hasta el año de 1797. Brujas, Paris, Desclée, de Brouwer, 1939.

Besson, Juan. Historia del Estado Zulia. Maracaibo, Editorial Hermanos Belloso Rossell, 1943.

Betancourt, Rómulo. Posición y doctrina. Caracas, Editorial Cordillera, 1959.

Betancourt, Rómulo. Rómulo Betancourt: pensamiento y acción. México, 1951.

Betancourt, Rómulo. Venezuela: política y petróleo. México, Fondo de Cultura Económica, 1956.

Bierck, Harold A., Jr. Vida pública de Don Pedro Gual. Caracas, Ministerio de Educación Nacional, Dirección de Cultura, 1947.

Bingham, Hiram. The journal of an Expedition across Venezuela and Colombia, 1906-1907. New Haven, Yale University Press, 1909.

Blanco Fombona, Rufino. El conquistador español del siglo XVI. Caracas, Ediciones Edime, 1956.

Bolívar, Simón. Cartas. Caracas, Ministerio de Educación, 1958.

Bolívar, Simón. Obras completas. Habana, Editorial Lex, 1950. 3 vols.

Bolívar Coronado, R. El Llanero. Buenos Aires, Editorial Venezuela, 1947.

Bonilla, Frank and José A. Silva Michelena. Studying the Venezuelan Polity. Cambridge, Massachusetts Institute of Technology; Caracas, Centro de Estudios del Desarrollo, Universidad Central de Venezuela, 1966.

Botero Saldarriaga, Roberto. Francisco Antonio Zea. Bogotá, Ediciones del Consejo, 1945.

Briceño, Manuel. Los "ilustres"; ó la estafa de los Guzmanes. Caracas, Ediciones Fe y Cultura, 195-.

Briceño Iragorry, Mario. Obras selectas. Madrid, Ediciones Edime, 1954.

Brito Figueroa, Federico. La estructura social y demográfica de Venezuela colonial. Caracas, Ediciones Historia, 1961.

Brito Figueroa, Federico. Historia económica y social de Venezuela. Caracas, Dirección de Cultura, Universidad Central de Venezuela, 1966. 2 vols.

Buitrón, Aníbal. Causas y efectos del exodo rural en Venezuela--Efectos económicos y sociales de las inmigraciones en Venezuela--Las inmigraciones en Venezuela. Washington, D. C., Pan American Union, 1956.

Caldera Rodríguez, Rafael. Idea de una sociología venezolana. Caracas, Libería y Editorial Alma Mater, 1954.

Cárdenas, Rodolfo José. La insurrección popular en Vene-
    zuela. Caracas, Ediciones Catatumbo, 1961.

Carrillo Moreno, José. Matías Salazar. Caracas, Ediciones
    Garrido, 1954.

Castro, Américo. La realidad histórica de España. México,
    Editorial Porrúa, 1954.

Chaves, Fernando Luis. Geografía agraria de Venezuela.
    Caracas, Ediciones de la Biblioteca, Universidad
    Central de Venezuela, 1963.

Clagett, Helen L. A Guide to the Law and Legal Literature
    of Venezuela. Washington, D. C., Library of Con-
    gress, 1947.

Clemente Travieso, Carmen. Mujeres venezolanas y otros
    reportajes. Caracas, Avila Gráfica, 1951.

Cleveland, Grover. The Venezuelan Boundary Controversy.
    Princeton, Princeton University Press, 1913.

Consejo Venezolano del Niño. El consejo venezolano del
    niño y la obra promenor en Venezuela. Caracas,
    Editorial Sucre, 1955.

Cova, Jesús Antonio. Archivo del Mariscal, Juan Crisósto-
    mo Falcón. Caracas, Imprenta Nacional, 1957-1960.
    5 vols.

Cova, Jesús Antonio. Don Simón Rodríguez, maestro y
    filósofo revolucionario. 3d ed. Caracas, J. Villegas,
    1954.

Cova, Jesús Antonio. Geografía física y política de Vene-
    zuela. Caracas, Elite, 1936.

Cova, Jesús Antonio. Guzmán Blanco, su vida y su obra.
    Caracas, Avila Gráfica, 1950.

Cova, Jesús Antonio. Miranda, el Venezolano del "fuego
    sagrado." Caracas, Tipografía Vargas, 1949.

Cova, Jesús Antonio. Resumen de la historia de Venezuela,
    desde el descubrimiento hasta nuestros días. 11th
    ed. Caracas, Editorial "Las Novedades," 1943.

Crist, Raymond E. Venezuela. Garden City, Doubleday, 1959.

Dalton, Leonard Victor. Venezuela. London, T. F. Unwin, 1912.

Dávila, Vicente. Diccionario biográfico de ilustres próceres de la independencia suramericana. Caracas, 1924-1926. 2 vols.

Depons, François. Viaje a la parte oriental de tierra firme. Caracas, Tipografía Americana, 1930.

Diament de Sujo, Clara. Art in Latin America Today: Venezuela. Translated by Ralph E. Dimmick and William McLeod Rivera. Washington, D. C., Pan American Union, 1962.

Díaz Sánchez, Ramón. Guzmán, eclipse de una ambición de poder. Caracas, Ministerio de Educación Nacional, Dirección de Cultura, 1950.

Diccionario biográfico de Venezuela. Madrid, Blass Tipografía, 1953.

Egaña, Manuel R. Tres décadas de producción petrolera. Caracas, Tipografía Americana, 1947.

Epistolaria de la primera república. Caracas, Academia Nacional de la Historia, Sesquicentenario de la Independencia, 1960. 2 vols.

Felice Cardot, Carlos. La rebelión de Andresote (Valles del Yaracuy, 1730-1733). Caracas, Imprenta Nacional, 1952.

Fergusson, Erna. Venezuela. London, Knopf, 1942.

Fernández, Pablo Emilio. Gómez, el rehabilitator. Caracas, J. Villegas, 1956.

Fernández y Fernández, Ramón. Reforma agraria en Venezuela. Caracas, Tipografía Vargas, 1948.

Ferrer Faria, Ivan. Ensayo sociológico de un medio rural concentrado venezolano. Maracaibo, Tipografía Cervantes, 1957.

129

Friedmann, John. Regional Development Policy; a Case Study
of Venezuela. Cambridge, Massachusetts Institute of
Technology Press, 1966.

Friedmann, John. Venezuela: from Doctrine to Dialogue.
Syracuse, N.Y., Syracuse University Press, 1965.

Gabaldón Márquez, Joaquín. Archivos de una inquietud venezolana. Caracas, Ediciones Edime, 1955.

Gallegos, Rómulo et al. Rómulo Betancourt: interpretación
de su doctrina popular y democrática. Caracas,
SUMA, 1958.

Gandía, Enrique de. Límites de las gobernaciones sud ame-
ricanas en el siglo XVI. Buenos Aires, A. García
Santos, 1933.

García Chuecos, Héctor. La Capitanía General de Venezuela.
Caracas, C.A. Artes Gráficas, 1945.

García Chuecos, Héctor. Catálogo de documentos referentes
a historia de Venezuela y de América existentes en el
Archivo Nacional de Washington. Caracas, 1950.

García Chuecos, Héctor. Estudios de historia colonial venezolana. Caracas, Tipografía Americana, 1937-1938.
2 vols.

García Chuecos, Héctor. Historia documental de Venezuela.
Caracas, Editorial Rex, 1957.

García Chuecos, Héctor. Siglo XVIII venezolano. Caracas,
Ediciones Edime, 1956.

Gil Fortoul, José. Historia constitucional de Venezuela.
4th ed. Caracas, Ministerio de Educación, Dirección
de Cultura y Bellas Artes, Comisión Editora de las
Obras Completas de José Gil Fortoul, 1953-1955. 3
vols.

Gilmore, Robert L. Caudillism and Militarism in Venezuela,
1810-1910. Athens, Ohio University Press, 1964.

Goetz, Delia. Education in Venezuela. Washington, D.C.,
Government Printing Office, 1948.

González Baquero, R. Análisis del proceso histórico de la educación, urbana (1870-1932) y de la educación rural (1932-1957). Caracas, Facultad de Filosofía y Letras, Universidad Central de Venezuela, 1962.

González Guiñán, Francisco. Hallazgo del acta solemne de independencia de Venezuela y de otras actas originales del Congreso constituyente de 1811. Valencia, Imprenta del Estado, 1908.

González Guiñán, Francisco. Historia contemporánea de Venezuela. Caracas, Tipografía Empresa El Cojo, 1909-1925. 15 vols.

González Guiñán, Francisco. Historia del gobierno de la aclamación, período constitucional de Venezuela, presidido por el general Guzmán Blanco (1886-1887). Caracas, Tipografía Universal, 1899.

González Guiñán, Francisco. Historia del gobierno del doctor J. P. Rojas Paúl, presidente de los Estados Unidos de Venezuela en el período constitucional de 1888 á 1890. Valencia, Imprenta de "La Voz Pública," 1891.

Graham, Robbert, B. C. José Antonio Páez. Philadelphia, Macrae, Smith, 1929.

Griffin, Charles C. Los temas sociales y económicos en la época de la independencia. Caracas, Editorial Arte, 1962.

Grisanti, Angel. Emparán y el golpe de estado de 1810. Caracas, Tipografía Lux, 1960.

Grisanti, Angel. Resumen histórico de la instrucción pública en Venezuela. Bogotá, Editorial Iqueima, 1950.

Gumilla, P. Joseph. El Orinoco ilustrado. Bogotá, Editorial ABC, 1944.

Hasbrouck, Alfred. Foreign Legionaires in the Liberation of Spanish South America. New York, Columbia University Press, 1928.

Hill, George W. El Estado Sucre: sus recursos humanos. Caracas, Universidad Central de Venezuela, 1961.

131

Hill, George W., José M. Silva, and Ruth Hill. La vida rural en Venezuela. Caracas, Tipografía Vargas, 1960.

Hill, Howard C. Roosevelt and the Caribbean. Chicago, University of Chicago Press, 1927.

Humboldt, Alexander von. Personal Narrative of Travels to the Equinoctial Regions of the New Continent During the Years 1799-1804. Translated by Helen Maria Williams. London, Longman, Hurst, Rees, Orme, and Brown, 1814-1829. 7 vols.

Hussey, Roland Dennis. The Caracas Company, 1728-1784. London, Oxford University Press, 1934.

International Bank for Reconstruction and Development. The Economic Development of Venezuela. Edited by H. David Davis. Baltimore Johns Hopkins University Press, 1961.

Ireland, Gordon. Boundaries, Possessions and Conflicts in South America. Cambridge, Harvard University Press, 1938.

Jankus, Alfred P. and Neil M. Malloy. Venezuela: Land of Opportunity. New York, Pageant Press, 1956.

Johnson, John J. The Role of the Military in Under-Developed Countries. Princeton, Princeton University Press, 1962.

Kirchhoff, Herbert. Venezuela. Buenos Aires, Kraft, 1956.

Lavin, John. A Halo for Gómez. New York, Pageant Press, 1954.

Lecuna, Vicente. Bolívar y el arte militar formada sobre documentos, sin utilizar consejas ni versiones impropias. New York, Colonial Press, 1955.

Lecuna, Vicente. Crónica razonada de las guerras de Bolívar. New York, Colonial Press, 1950. 3 vols.

Lecuna, Vicente. Proclamas y discursos del Libertador. Caracas, 1939.

Lecuna, Vicente. La revolución de Queipa. Caracas, Ediciones Garrido, 1954.

Level de Goda, Luis. Historia contemporánea de Venezuela (1858-1886). Barcelona, 1893. 2 vols.

Lieuwen, Edwin. Generals vs. Presidents. New York, Frederick A. Praeger, 1964.

Lieuwen, Edwin. Petroleum in Venezuela: a History. Berkeley, California University Press, 1954.

Lieuwen, Edwin. Venezuela. 2d ed. London, Oxford University Press, 1965.

López Contreras, Eleazar. Páginas para la historia militar de Venezuela. Caracas, 1945.

López Contreras, Eleazar. El triunfo de la verdad. México, Edición Genio Latero, 1949.

Lossada Piñeres, Juan A. Hombres notables de la revolución del 92 en Venezuela. Caracas, Imprenta y Litografía Nacional, 1893-1895. 2 vols.

Luciani, Jorge. La dictadura perpétua de Gómez y sus adversarios. Caracas, Cooperativa de Artes Gráficas, 1936.

Lugo, Francisco A. Pérez Jiménez; fuerza creadora. 2d ed. Caracas, Imprenta Nacional, 1954.

Luzardo, Rodolfo. Notas histórico-económicas, 1928-1963. Caracas, Editorial Sucre, 1963.

Luzardo, Rodolfo. Venezuela: business and finances. Englewood Cliffs, Prentice Hall, 1957.

Maby, A. C. Venezuela: Economic and Commercial Conditions. London, His Majesty's Stationary Office, 1951.

Madariaga, Salvador de. Simón Bolívar. México, Editorial Hermes, 1951. 2 vols.

Magallanes, Manuel Vicente. Partidos políticos venezolanos. Caracas, Tipografía Vargas, 1959.

Los manifiestos de la liberación: recopilación de los manifiestos que circularon clandestinamente desde el 1°
hasta el 23 el enero de 1958, día de la liberación
venezolana. Caracas, Editorial Pensamiento Vivo,
1958.

Marsland, William D. Venezuela Through its History. New
York, Crowell, 1954.

Martz, John D. Acción Democrática: Evolution of a Modern
Political Party in Venezuela. Princeton, Princeton
University Press, 1966.

Masur, Gerhard. Simón Bolívar. Albuquerque, New Mexico
University Press, 1948.

Mecham, J. L. Church and State in Latin America. Chapel
Hill, University of North Carolina Press, 1934.

Medina, José Ramón. Examen de la posea venezolana
contemporánea. Caracas, Colección "Letras Venezolanas, " 1956.

Miranda, Francisco de. Archivo. Caracas, Editorial Sur
América, 1929.

Montenegro y Colón, Feliciano. Historia de Venezuela.
Caracas, Academia Nacional de la Historia, 1960. 2
vols.

Morón, Guillermo. A History of Venezuela. Translated by
John Street. London, George Allen and Unwin, 1964.

Morón, Guillermo. Los orígenes históricos de Venezuela.
Madrid, Consejo Superior de Investigaciones Científi-
cas, Instituto "Gonzalo Fernández de Oviedo, " 1954.

Navarro, Nicolás Eugenio. Anales eclesiásticos venezolanos.
2d ed. Caracas, Tipografía Americana, 1951.

Navarro, Nicolás Eugenio. El cabildo metropolitano de Caracas y la guerra de emanicipación. Caracas, Academia Nacional de la Historia, 1960.

Navarro, Nicolás Eugenio. La iglesia y masonería en Venezuela. Caracas, Editorial Sur América, 1928.

Neuberger, Otto. A Guide to the Official Publications of the Other American Republics. XIX: Venezuela. Washington, D. C., Library of Congress, 1948.

O'Leary, Daniel Florencio. Memorias: narración. Caracas, Imprenta Nacional, 1952. 3 vols.

Oropesa, Juan. 4 siglos de historia venezolana. Caracas, Libería y Editorial del Maestro, 1947.

Ovalles, Víctor Manuel. Llaneros auténticos. Caracas, Editorial Bolívar, 1935.

Oviedo y Baños, José de. Historia de la conquista y población de la provincia de Venezuela. Madrid, L. Navarro, 1885.

Pachano, Jacinto Regino. Biografía del Mariscal Juan C. Falcón. Paris, 1876.

Páez, José Antonio. Archivo del general José Antonio Páez, documentación del Archivo Nacional de Colombia. Bogotá, Editorial "El Gráfico, " 1939-1957. 2 vols.

Páez, José Antonio. Autobiografía. New York, H. R. Elliot and Co., 1946.

Paredes, Antonio. Como llegó Cipriano Castro al poder. 2d ed. Caracas, Ediciones Garrido, 1954.

Pareja, José and Paz Soldán. Juan Vicente Gómez, un fenómeno telúrico. Caracas, Editorial Avila Gráfica, 1951.

Parra, Francisco J. Doctrinas de la cancillería venezolana. New York, Las Américas, 1952. 2 vols.

Parra León, Caracciolo. La instrucción en Caracas, 1567-1725. Caracas, Parra León Hermanos, 1932.

Parra Pérez, Caracciolo. Historia de la primera república de Venezuela. 2d ed. Caracas, Academia Nacional de la Historia, 1959. 2 vols.

Parra Pérez, Caracciolo. Mariño y la independencia de Venezuela. Madrid, Ediciones Cultura Hispánica, 1954-1956. 5 vols.

Parra Pérez, Caracciolo. Mariño y las guerras civiles. Madrid, Ediciones Cultura Hispánica, 1958-1960. 3 vols.

Parra Pérez, Caracciolo. El régimen español en Venezuela. 2d ed. Madrid, Cultura Hispánica, 1964.

Pattee, Richard. El catolicismo contemporáneo en Hispano América. Buenos Aires, Editorial Fides, 1948.

Pensamiento político venezolano del siglo XIX. Caracas, Ediciones Presidencia de la República, 1928. 15 vols.

Pereira, Pedro N. En la prisión. Caracas, Editorial Avila Gráfica, 1952.

Pérez Jiménez, Marcos. Pensamiento político del Presidente de Venezuela. Caracas, Imprenta Nacional, 1954.

Picón Febres, Gonzalo. Don Simón Rodríguez, maestro del Libertador. Caracas, Cooperativa de Artes Gráficas, 1939.

Picón Febres, Gonzalo. La literatura venezolana en el siglo XIX. Caracas, "Empresa el Cojo, " 1906.

Picón Rivas, Ulises. Indice constitucional de Venezuela. Caracas, Editorial Elite, 1944.

Picón Salas, Mariano. Comprensión de Venezuela. Madrid, 1955.

Picón Salas, Mariano. Los días de Cipriano Castro (historia venezolana del 1900). Caracas, Ediciones Garrido, 1953.

Picón Salas, Mariano. Formación y proceso de la literatura venzolana. Caracas, Impresores Unidos, 1940.

Picón Salas, Mariano et al. Venezuela independiente 1810-1960. Caracas, Fundación Eugenio Mendoza, 1962.

Planchart, Enrique. La pintura en Venezuela. Caracas, 1956.

Plaza, Eduardo R.   La contribución de Venezuela al Pan
Americanismo durante el período 1939-1943.   Caracas, 1945.

Pocaterra, José R.   Memorias de un venezolano de la decadencia.   Caracas, Editorial Elite, 1936.   2 vols.

Pogue, Joseph E.   Oil in Venezuela.   New York, Chase National Bank, 1949.

Polanco Martínez, Tomás.   Esbozo sobre historia económica
venezolana.   2d ed.   Madrid, Ediciones Guadarrama,
1960.   2 vols.

Prieto Figueroa, Luis Beltrán.   De una educación de castas
a una educación de masas.   Habana, Editorial Lex,
1951.

Ramos, Arthur.   Las culturas negras en el nuevo mundo.
México, Fondo de Cultura Económica, 1943.

Rangel, Domingo Alberto.   La industrialización de Venezuela.
Caracas, Pensamienta Viva, 1958.

Rangel, Domingo Alberto.   La revolución de las fantasias.
Caracas, Ediciones ofidi, 1966.

Robertson, William Spence.   The Life of Miranda.   Chapel
Hill, University of North Carolina Press, 1929.   2
vols.

Rodulfo Cortés, Santos.   Antología documental de Venezuela,
1492-1900.   Caracas, 1960.

Rojas, Arístides.   Orígenes venezolanos.   Caracas, 1891.

Rojas, Wilson J.   Razón y objectivos para la vigencia de la
reforma agraria en Venezuela.   Caracas, Instituto
Agrario Nacional, 1962.

Rondón Márquez, Rafael Angel.   La esclavitud en Venezuela.
Caracas, Tipografía Garrido, 1954.

Rondón Márquez, Rafael Angel.   Guzmán Blanco, "el autócra-
ta civilizador. "   2d ed.   Madrid, García Vicente,
1952.

Roscio, Juan Germán. Obras. Caracas, Publicaciones de la Secretaría General de la Décima Conferencia Interamericana, 1953. 3 vols.

Rourke, Thomas. Gómez; Tyrant of the Andes. New York, Morrow, 1941.

Rourke, Thomas. Man of Glory, Simón Bolívar. New York, Morrow, 1942.

Royal Institute of International Affairs. Venezuela; a Brief Political and Economic Survey. London, 1958.

Salas, Julio C. Etnología e historia de tierra firme. Madrid, Editorial América, 191-.

Sánchez, Manuel Segundo. Bibliografía venezolanista: contribución al conocimiento de los libros extranjeros relativos a Venezuela y sus grandes hombres. Caracas, Empresa El Cojo, 1914.

Sangróniz y Castro, José A. Familias coloniales de Venezuela. Caracas, Editorial Bolívar, 1943.

Serrano, José Aniceto. Violencia ejercida por el poder ejecutiva de la República de la Venezuela en 1848 contra la cámara de representantes proceder de algunas provincias para salvar las instituciones. Santo Domingo, 1878.

Shoup, Carl et al. The Fiscal System of Venezuela. Baltimore, Johns Hopkins University Press, 1959.

Silva Guillén, Rafael. La reforma agraria en Venezuela. Caracas, Instituto Agrario Nacional, 1962.

Simón, Fray Pedro. Noticias historiales de las conquistas de tierre firme en las Indias Occidentales. Bogotá, M. Rivas, 1882-1892. 3 pts. in 5 vols.

Siso, Carlos. La formación del pueblo venezolano: estudios sociológicos. New York, Horizon House, 1941.

Siso Martínez, J. M. Historia de Venezuela. México, Editorial "Yocoima," 1957.

Smith, T. Lynn. Latin American Population Studies. Gainesville, University of Florida Press, 1961.

Sojo, Juan Pablo. Temas y apuntes afro-venezolanos. Caracas, Tipografía La Nación, 1943.

Soto, César Humberto. Personajes célebres de Venezuela. Caracas, Bibliografía Cecilo Acosta, 1946.

Steward, Julian H. Handbook of South American Indians. Vol. IV. Washington, D. C., Government Printing Office, 1948.

Steward, Julian H. and L. Faron. Native Peoples of South America. New York, McGraw-Hill, 1959.

Sucre-Reyes, José. Le système colonial espagnol dans l'ancien Venezuela. Paris, Rousseau and Cie., 1939.

Tannenbaum, Frank. Slave and Citizen: the Negro in the Americas. New York, Knopf, 1947.

Tarnói, Ladislao. El nuevo ideal nacional de Venezuela; vida y obra de Marcos Pérez Jiménez. Madrid, Ediciones Verdad, 1954.

Testimonio de la república en Venezuela 1° de enero-23 de julio, 1958. Caracas, Tipografía Vargas, 1958.

Thorning, Joseph F. Miranda, World Citizen. Gainesville, University of Florida Press, 1952.

Thurber, Orray E. The Venezuelan Question; Castro and the Asphalt Trust from Official Records. New York, 1907.

Toro, Fermín. Reflexiones sobre la ley de 10 de abril de 1834 y otras obras. Caracas, Ministerio de Educación Nacional, Dirección de Cultura, 1941.

Tosta, Virgilio. El caudillismo según once autores venezolanos. Caracas, Tipografía Garrido, 1954.

Tosta García, Francisco. Costumbres caraqueños. Caracas, 1882-1883. 2 vols. in 1.

Trend, John Brande. Bolívar and the Independence of Spanish America. London, Published by Hodder and

Stoughton for the English Universities Press, 1946.

Umaña Bernal, José. Testimonio de la revolución en Venezuela. Caracas, Tipografía Vargas, 1958.

United States. Army. Area Handbook for Venezuela. Washington, D. C., Government Printing Office, 1964.

United States. Commission to Investigate and Report on the True Divisional Line Between Venezuela and British Guiana. Report and Accompanying Papers. Washington, D. C., Government Printing Office, 1896-1897. 8 vols.

United States. Congress. 86th. 2nd Session. Senate. Committee on Foreign Relations. Latin America: Venezuela, Brazil, Peru, Bolivia and Panama. Washington, D. C., Government Printing Office, 1960.

United States. Department of State. Correspondence Relating to Wrongs Done to American Citizens by the Government of Venezuela. Washington, D. C., Government Printing Office, 1908.

United States. Library of Congress. List of Writings on the Venezuela Case, 1902-1903. Washington, D. C., Government Printing Office, 1908.

Uslar Pietri, Arturo. De una a otra Venezuela. Caracas, Ediciones Mesa Redonda, 1950.

Uslar Pietri, Arturo. Letras y hombres de Venezuela. México, Fondo de Cultura Económica, 1948.

Uslar Pietri, Arturo. Materiales para la estructura de Venezuela. Caracas, Ediciones Orinoco, 1959.

Uslar Pietri, Arturo. Obras selectas. Madrid, Ediciones Edime, 1953.

Uslar Pietri, Arturo. Sumario de economía venezolana. 2d ed. Caracas, Fundación Eugenio Mendoza, 1958.

Uslar Pietri, Juan. Historia de la rebelión popular de 1814. Paris, Ediciones Soberbia, 1954.

Vallenilla Lanz, Laureano. Cesarismo democrático. 3d ed.

Caracas, Tipografía Garrido, 1952.

Vallenilla Lanz, Laureano. Disgregación e integración. Caracas, Tipografía Universal, 1930.

Venezuela. Historia oficial de la discusión entre Venezuela y la Gran Bretaña sobre sus límites en la Guayana. New York, Weiss, 1896.

Venezuela. Consejo de Bienestar Rural. Problemas económicos y sociales de los Andes venezolanos. Caracas, 1955-1956. 2 vols.

Venezuela. Ministerio de Relaciones Exteriores. El libro amarillo. Caracas, 1894.

Venezuela. Universidad Central. Facultad de Humanidades y Educación. Historia de la cultura en Venezuela. Caracas, Instituto de Filosofía, Facultad de Humanidades y Educación, Universidad Central de Venezuela, 1955-1956. 2 vols.

Vigas, Andrés. Perfiles parlementarias. Caracas, 1893.

Vila, Marco Aurelio. Geografía de Venezuela. 7th ed. Caracas, Fundación Eugenio Mendoza, 1961.

Villanueva, Laureano. Vida del valiente ciudadano general Ezequiel Zamora. Caracas, Imprenta Federación, 1898.

Ward, Edward. The New El Dorado: Venezuela. London, Hale, 1957.

Watters, Mary. A History of the Church in Venezuela 1810-1930. Chapel Hill, University of North Carolina Press, 1933.

Waugh, Elizabeth. Simón Bolívar. New York, Macmillan, 1947.

Whitaker, Arthur P. The United States and South America: the Northern Republics. Cambridge, Harvard University Press, 1948.

Wilgus, Alva Curtis (ed.). The Caribbean: Venezuelan development. Gainesville, University of Florida Press, 1963.

Wilgus, Alva Curtis (ed.). South American Dictators During the First Century of Independence. Washington, D.C., George Washington University Press, 1937.

Wise, George S. El caudillo; a Portrait of Antonio Guzmán Blanco. New York, Columbia University Press, 1951.

Wohlrabe, Raymond A. The Land and People of Venezuela. Philadelphia, Lippincott, 1959.

Yañes, Francisco Javier. Compendio de la historia de Venezuela desde su descubrimiento y conquista hasta que se declaró estado independiente. Caracas, Editorial Elite, 1944.

Yañes, Francisco Javier. Historia de la provincia de Cumaná en la transformación política de Venezuela desde el día 27 de abril de 1810 hasta el presente año de 1821. Caracas, Ministerio de Educación Nacional, Dirección de Cultura y Bellas Artes, 1949.

Yañes, Francisco Javier. Historia de Margarita. Caracas, Ministerio de Educación Nacional, Dirección de Cultura, 1948.

Yañes, Francisco Javier. Manual político del venezolano. Caracas, Academia Nacional de la Historia, 1959.

Zuloaga, Guillermo. Geografía petrolera de Venezuela. Caracas, Cromotip, 1960.

Zuloaga, Guillermo. A Geographical Glimpse of Venezuela. Caracas, Cromotip, 1957.

Zweig, Stefan. Américo Vespucio. Buenos Aires, Editorial Claridad, 1942.

142